A RATIONAL FAITH:

Essays in Honor of Levi A. Olan

A RATIONAL FAITH:

Essays in Honor of Levi A. Olan

Edited by
Jack Bemporad

KTAV PUBLISHING HOUSE, INC.
NEW YORK
1977

Library of Congress Cataloging in Publication Data
Main entry under title:

A Rational faith.

Includes bibliographical references.
CONTENTS: Atlas, S. On the relation between subject
and object.—Bamberger, B. Religion and the arts.—
Bemporad, J. Man, God, and history. [etc.]
1. Judaism—History—Addresses, essays, lectures. 2.
Philosophy—Addresses, essays, lectures. 3. Olan, Levi
Arthur, 1903-   I. Olan, Levi Arthur, 1903-   —Ad-
dresses, essays, lectures. II. Bemporad, Jack.
BM42.R35   296   77-13626
ISBN 0-87068-448-5

TABLE OF CONTENTS

ACKNOWLEDGMENT

The publication of this book was made possible through the generosity of the Temple Emanu-El Sisterhood and Temple Emanu-El Brotherhood, Dallas, Texas, as an expression of their appreciation and devotion to Rabbi Emeritus Levi A. Olan, in recognition of his outstanding contributions to Temple Emanu-El, the community, and Reform Judaism.

PREFACE

The essays in this volume written by friends and colleagues of Rabbi Levi Olan are published in his honor and as a tribute to his signal contribution to the theory and practice of Reform Judaism.

They cover a range of topics and reflect the many areas of his interest and the varied contributions he has made. A special summing up by Rabbi Olan is included which outlines his most recent reflections.

Those of us who know Rabbi Olan have found ourselves enlightened by his perception, uplifted by his wisdom and inspired by his humanity. He possesses a rare talent that enables him to impart his great store of knowledge with depth and captivating wit. To him we are indebted for his constant efforts to foster our well-being, and so feeling, we are most gratified to be able in some small measure to recognize his gifts to us through this volume.

The editor wishes to express his personal thanks to Dr. Martin Yaffe of the Department of Philosophy, North Texas State University, for his kind editorial assistance.

J.B.

INTRODUCTION

GERALD J. KLEIN

Levi Olan will rejoice in this volume. He has spent a lifetime seeking the ideas and thoughts of his scholar-friends. They can be sure that he has, he does, and he will read their writings. They can be sure that he is interested in them, their families, their frustrations, and the way they spend their leisure hours. He is known (envied!) for his lifetime ability to find library corners in which to study and write, but he has never become "ivory tower." Indeed, there is evidence that, surrounded by books and pencils, he searches as much for insights and approaches to human ills as he does for philosophical and theological stimulation. He has written on immortality, but his yearning is not for the *Yeshiva Shel Ma-aloh* (the "academy on high"). His idea of heaven has been that table in the library with an occasional welcome interruption from a friend—even a friend in need.

It is not necessary, therefore, to strike a balance sheet of Olan accomplishment. He has always eschewed the bookkeeping approach to human relations—what I have done for you and what you have done for me. He has had more than his share of honors. He has been at ease in the White House, the board room, and the Chasidic *shtibl.* He has heard a spokesman from Southern Methodist University refer to him as a "rare combination of talent and devotion," an Austin College presenter extol his "articulate scholarship," and a Hebrew Union College-

Jewish Institute of Religion president proclaim him "a keen interpreter of Jewish thought and forceful preacher." All three of these schools have conferred honorary doctorates upon him. The six years that Levi Olan served as a regent of The University of Texas System with distinction and achievement are an indication that the college campus is a natural environment for his personality and his life style. Institutions of higher learning have recognized this, and he has become known as a challenging and sought-after teacher of the changing facets of the subject of the nature of man.

The year 1929 has become symbolic for Levi Olan. In this year of the Great Depression, he became a rabbi. In 1929 Dr. David Lefkowitz of Dallas, Texas, whom he was destined to succeed, was serving as president of the Central Conference of American Rabbis, a significant post to which Rabbi Olan was elected in 1967. He refers to this duality of circumstances often in his preaching. Nineteen twenty-nine in Worcester, Massachusetts, was the starting point of the Olan style of preaching, always emphasizing "what is and hadn't ought to be." This characteristic, which has become a sacred compulsion to explore existing inhumanities and to condemn inequalities, has continued to this day.

Twenty years after 1929, Levi Olan came to Dallas, Texas. He became not only rabbi to Temple Emanu-El, but in many ways religious leader of the community. What momentous and traumatic events have occurred during his Dallas years! Whether it was the 1954 desegregation decision of the United States Supreme Court, the Vietnam War, the assassination in Dallas of John F. Kennedy, it was to Rabbi Olan that the people of Dallas turned for insight, analysis, and guidance. To this day the question "What does Rabbi Olan think?" is an important and natural one.

His scholarship has been in the field of theology and philosophy. In this volume he contributes "A Preliminary Summing Up" to which the reader can turn. Those of us who have heard him as well as read him, have a distinct advantage. He captures nuances and conveys interpretation in his teaching and preaching that are unique and are not easily transmitted to the printed page.

There is something just right about this Festschrift for Levi A. Olan. A Festschrift is, after all, just a book—and books, in the Olan view, are what it's all about. This is a book in honor of Levi A. Olan, published by a grateful congregation which he has served well. A book to be placed among the thousands and thousands he has read and from which he has taught. May this book be for him something of a *Sefer Chayim*—a book of life and sustained vigor.

REFLECTIONS ON THE RELATION OF SUBJECT AND OBJECT

SAMUEL ATLAS

The meeting of subject and object is a cognitive act of life; the idea of their unity is an act transcending life.

THE idea generally prevailing in the treatment of the question concerning the relation between "subject" and "object" is grounded in the assumption that the subject and the object are entities per se, i.e., that they are entities existing in themselves. The problem of the relation between them is therefore generally taken to be a question concerning the relationship obtaining between two set and fixed entities; the "actual" entities of subject and object are thus considered to be prior to the relation obtaining between them. This approach to the problem is rooted in a groundless dualism which will not stand the light of critical examination.

A critical analysis of the real meaning of the concepts of subject and object, and of the problem of their relation to one another, must lead to a reversal of the order of priority: the *relation* must not be thought of as posterior to the *entities* of subject and object, but as prior to them. There is no subject *in itself*, and no object *in itself*, but in every object there are subjective elements, and every subject is related to objects.

1

Subject and object are thus inseparable from one another: they are mutually interdependent. Subjective forms of thought are inherent in the cognition of any object, and the process of cognition is always related to an object.

By analysis of the cognitive act we can never obtain the object per se, entirely abstracted from the forms of thought and perception which encompass the subject. Nor, for that matter, can we arrive at consciousness per se, entirely abstracted from the objects cognized. Subject per se and object per se are thus mere abstractions: they are not real. In reality, subject and object are always conjoined. Every phenomenon of reality, every appearance, is both subjective and objective. When we say "something appears" or "an object appears" we mean: (a) that there is an object, which appears, and (b) that there is a consciousness to which it appears. Thus, an object is always an object for a subject, and a subject is always related to objects. In other words, a thing is always a thing for a consciousness, and consciousness is always an awareness of a thing.

Now, in order to be more precise instead of gratuitously positing a dualism of subject and object as realities per se, we can only speak of a relation between two unknown quantities: for subject per se and object per se are totally unknown quantities. We can say, therefore, that in every reality, in every appearance, there is an implicit relation to two ideal limits (two "ideas," in the Kantian sense): one limit is the idea of object per se, and the other is the idea of subject, i.e., consciousness, per se. In every actual reality, however, and in every actual appearance, there is a conjunction of the subjective and the objective—that is to say, every actual object is a point of convergence of the subjective and the objective. Subject and object in themselves, as unknown quantities, are to be designated as X.

The historical process of the struggle of man for the cognition of the phenomena of the world is in its very essence a striving for order, greater objectivity, and greater unity. "Greater objectivity," however, still implies the presence of some subjectivity. In every stage of the endless growth and development of scientific thought—which tries to establish greater objectivity—there are still contained some subjective elements, without which cognition is impossible. An objective unity which is a thing in itself, i.e., which is purely object and no subject, is nonexistent; it is a mere idea. Moreover, such an objective unity has no meaning whatsoever, since an object is always an object for consciousness, and an objective unity abstracted from its relation to a consciousness is meaningless. In the search for such an imaginary reality—an absolute object—we lose sight of the real nature of the objective unity as it is presented by the scientific process. Critical philosophy, however, has realized this central idea, namely, that there is no subject without object and no object without subject; it is thus a philosophy of experience. The idealism of critical philosophy is actually a true realism. The real meaning of critical philosophy, as formulated by Kant, consists in the realization that the rigid and fixed dualism of subject and object must be replaced by a dualism of relation: namely, that every object cognized contains a relation of subject and object as two abstract ideas, i.e., as two ideal limits.

We should acknowledge that the absolute dichotomy of subject, on the one hand, and object, on the other, as if they were real and rigid entities in themselves, does not correspond to reality. We should recognize, instead, that in reality there is a dichotomy of two series of gradations or progressions: namely, that of objectivizations and that of subjectivizations. While the ideal goal and purpose of natural science is the attainment of absolute and pure objectivizations, the ideal goal of the study of the essence of consciousness should be the attainment of the pure self, the pure subjectivization. Psychology, however, as a science trying to determine the laws governing the association of ideas, emotions, and perceptions, is a natural science like any other. As such, the objects of psychology, as of any other natural science, represent a point of convergence between subject and object. The study of the pure self, i.e., the search for the constitutive forms of consciousness and the a priori elements of thought, is the subject matter of philosophy or of pure psychology. The latter should be clearly differentiated from psychology as a natural science. Pure objectivization as the ideal goal of physical science, and pure subjectivization as the ideal goal of pure psychology, are not meant in the sense of an attainable end which is to be achieved in the historical process of scientific investigation. They are merely meant to be limiting concepts. There is no conclusion of the series in one direction toward the absolute object or in the other direction toward the absolute subject. We are always in the midst of the series of gradations, the totality of which presents the continuous, eternal process of experience. The conception of an object in each stage of this endless series of gradations is objective (or, better, more objective), in comparison with a lower stage; and it is subjective in comparison with a higher stage of the scientific development.

Thus, for instance, when we see a certain color, red or blue, it is a real object for the simple, naive stage of cognition. By this act of perception, we believe we have recognized an identical object, a unity. It is not merely a subjective reaction of the perceiving subject, but a presentation of the object in itself. On a higher stage of cognition, however, we declare the perception of color is subjective. But even this scientific cognition of the object is constituted in a definite manner only for a subject constituted in a particular way. The qualities of color perceived by a subject are not the impressions of a selfsame and identical object, but they are the result of the reactions of the subject toward certain physical waves of light of a particular intensity. The cognition of the physical laws determining the perception of color may seem to be an objective cognition in comparison with which the previous prescientific cognition of the phenomenon of color is subjective. But even his scientific cognition of the essence of the perception of color is not the final and the completely fixed expression of its essence, since in the course of scientific development it may prove to be wrong and may be replaced by another theory. In comparison with a new theory of the physical laws determining the essence of color on a higher level, the present theory will be defined as subjective. Thus, every objective conception of an object is so only in comparison with a conception of the same object on a lower stage of cognition and consciousness; and it is in turn subjective when it is replaced by a new conception of the same object, in comparison with the latter. Thus, each attainment of objectivity in the process of cognition, viz., the cognition of an object as it actually is, can claim only comparative objectivity, relative to the previous stage of cognition. But since the process of scientific thought and cognition is a never-ending process, a process inconclusive and never static, each cognition of objectivity in the determination of an object can only be temporary and transient, for in relation to a higher stage of cognition, the one presently reached will prove to be subjective. Just as we can never definitely state of a cognition that it is absolutely objective, so can we never say of a stage of consciousness that it is absolutely and exclusively subjective. Even the lowest stage of consciousness contains some form of unification of the phenomena of experience with which it is confronted. And every act of unification of phenomena is an act of objectivization.

As to the most general functions of objectivization, such as the Kantian categories of thought, i.e., the categories of quantity, quality, relation, and modality, these are subjective in a particular sense of the term. They are the fundamental forms of the function of unification and identification of an object in general, since without them there would be no cognition of objects altogether. They are subjective not in the individual, psychological sense, but in a most general and compelling sense, relating to human consciousness as manifested in scientific thought. Being constitutive to human consciousness, these forms are subjective. They are also objective, inasmuch as only by means of these forms is the scientific cognition of objects by the human mind at all possible.

Thus, only the extreme limits on both sides of this endless series of gradations may be designated as objective or subjective. The absolute objectivization—in which the totality of the problems relating to an object has been completely mastered—constitutes the ultimate ideal limit of cognition. At such a stage of cognition, nothing is due to the subject. However, this requires a modification, for even the most general functions of unification of an object, such as the categories of thought, may be thought of as absolutely objective only under the assumption that they are metaphysical forms of thought per se, so that even the infinite, divine mind must think of objects in these forms. So long, however, as we have no guarantee that such a metaphysical assumption is warranted, even these general forms of thought, without which there can be no cognition of objects by the human mind altogether, are subjective. Consequently, even the most objective cognition by the human mind will still retain a minimal subjective element due to the necessary general functions of unification constitutive to human thought as such.

Habitually, the point of departure of the discussion concerning the relation obtaining between the subject and the object is the assumed dualism of the ego and the non-ego, the internal mental world as opposed to the external material world; for the critical idealist, however, such a starting point is a gratuitous and groundless dualism, for it dogmatically posits two independent realities per se before subjecting to a critical examination the very meaning of the terms "subject" and "object." As the material world is "outside" the subject in the sense of space, this initial dualism seems to take the spatial separation between the subject and the object as the fundamental basis for the dichotomy between them. But since space itself may be a subjective form of intuitive perception, as it is according to Kant, "outside" the subject in a spatial sense cannot be considered the basis for this dichotomy. We have, therefore, to consider the possibility of introducing another fundamental distinction by which the object and the subject can be defined. This consists of the following. In the light of the conception of the essence of cognition as consisting of the striving for greater objectivization, it can be justifiably stated that the object is the result of the act of objectivization. Since the object is not prior to the act of cognition but is, rather, its result, there are no objects—only objectivizations. The greater the objectivity in the cognition of a phenomenon, the closer is its approach to the ideal object. The attainment of the comprehension of an object as an absolute unity which is not the result of subjective impressions and perceptions, i.e., a unity which is not due to subjective perceptions, is objective; as such it can be designated as an absolute object. Those elements of cognition of an object which are due to the constitution of the subject, to its forms and modes of thought, are subjective. Subject and object cannot be defined separately and independently from one another; rather, each of them must be defined in relation to the other. It is generally assumed that in every cognition, those elements of cognition which are not attributable to the object are subjective, and those elements of the act of cognition which are not attributable to the subject are objective. Since, however, the exact assignment of elements to subject and object is actually impossible to achieve, for even the most objective elements of cognition are recognized as such by a consciousness constituted in a definite manner, we can designate as objective only the cognition of an object as an absolute unity in which all problems have been finally and definitely solved. Such a cognition, however, is an ideal goal to strive for, not a reality. The object and the subject cannot be set up as realities per se at the beginning of our analysis of the relation between them. The object is the result of an endless series of objectivizations, and the subject is the result of an endless series of subjectivizations, i.e., an endless process of abstraction of all references to objects. The object cannot stand at the beginning of the process of objectivization; it can only be the result of the sought-for end. Likewise, the subject cannot stand at the beginning of the process of subjectivization, but it can only be its result.

The idea of the identity of thought and being, of intellect and intelligible, first promulgated by Parmenides and Aristotle on the assumption of the rational foundation of reality and reoccurring in various contexts in the history of philosophy, adumbrates with some reservations the critical conception of the relation obtaining between subject and object. But considering the limited capacity of human understanding as restricted to the phenomena of experience, the identity of subject and object subsists only with regard to the intellectually integrated aspects of reality. Since, however, the objects are never comprehended in their entirety, as at every stage of the growth of scientific thought there arise problems challenging out integrated order and provoking our thought for further creative initiative, the identity of thought and being is never fully realized; its incompleteness is due to the inadequacy of our understanding comprehensibly to integrate the objects in their entirety. It is the fate of man that the fruit of our tree of knowledge is never full-grown. The meeting of subject and object is thus the result of a creative act of intellectual life of man struggling for order and unification of the phenomena, but realizing at the same time the incompleteness and the temporary nature of the partial correspondence between subject and object. The idea of the identity of thought and being, of subject and object, is therefore conceivable only as the ideal goal of attaining the solution to all problems and the total rationalization of the objects of reality, which is, however, an endless task the accomplishment of which can be conceived as an idea subsisting in infinity.

With reference to the idea of an infinite mind, in relation to which the totality of being is dissolvable in terms of intellectual integration, the identity of thought and being is fully realized. The idea of the identity of intellect, intelligible and intelligence is thus legitimate with reference to an infinite mind and has its systematic place in the world-view of dogmatic rationalism, which maintains that our cognition of the phenomena fully corresponds to the objects as they are in themselves (Spinoza, Hegel). But from the point of view of a critical system of thought, which realizes the piecemeal character of our knowledge of reality—that every new hypothesis is accompanied by the rise of new problems and that every novel synthesis aiming at the establishment of order generates new riddles and questions, with the result that our scientific knowledge is constantly being challenged and in a state of flux and change—the idea of the identity of thought and being can be considered only as a focus giving direction to our efforts and striving. While for man this identity is an infinite idea, it is a reality with regard to an infinite mind. As such it is an act surpassing experience; it is an act of transcendence like all metaphysical ideas, which have their root in the capacity of human reason to transcend itself.

The subject and object as entities per se are pure ideas in the Kantian sense. But in reality, i.e., in the historical process in which we are situated, every phenomenon as an object of cognition is both objective and subjective, for the subject and the object cannot be separated from each other. Instead of a dualism of two different entities, we should speak of a dualism of direction. The separation of subject and object from one another is, methodologically, a necessary procedure, for otherwise we will never gain clarity about the functions and limitations of our thinking capacity. A methodological distinction between subject and object means bringing into consciousness those elements and conditions present in the act of cognition which are to be attributed to the subject and those elements contained in the same cognition which refer to an objective reality. But a methodological distinction should not be hypostasized by transforming the elements of the distinction into two realities existing in themselves.

Thus, instead of conceiving subject and object as mere functions of objectivization and subjectivization standing always in a mutually inseparable relationship to one another, subject and object were considered as entirely separated from one another and posited as rigid and absolute realities, and the relation between them was conceived likewise to be a rigid relation between two existing independent entities. Thus, the real human being was torn into two: the mindless, soulless body, on the one hand, and the immaterial soul, the incorporeal mind, on the other. In other words, the unity of man was separated into two disparate parts, the "mindless" matter and the mind estranged from the material nature; mind and body, subject and object, appear thus as two strangers to one another.

In the same manner, the realm of nature and the ethical realm, namely, the understanding and the will, were separated and estranged from each other and treated as disparate realms of being. In the spirit of critical philosophy, we should clearly strive, on the one hand, for a methodological distinction between them, but at the same time recognize that in reality there is always a mutual relationship between understanding and the will, just as subject and object are always mutually related to one another. The idea of the "ought to be" which is the ideal determination of our will also determines our striving for greater objectivization in the cognition of nature, for without the idea of an absolute unity of the world, i.e., mastery of all the problems concerning the cognition of the realm of nature, the empirical process of acquiring scientific knowledge as manifested in history cannot be fully accounted for. The idea of the "ought to be" comprises also the idea of an absolute unity of the world which is the ideal goal in our striving for absolute objectivization of the objects of cognition.

Even though the idea of the "ought to be" was originally formulated as an ethical ideal, it has as well relevance and application to the theoretical comprehension of reality. For the ideal of an absolute unity, implying the total solution of all problems, is the goal dominating the cognitive process. In this sense, the "ought to be," namely, the absolute unity, is the overriding goal embracing the theoretical as well as the ethical realm.

Natural science is only one kind of objectivization, namely, the determination of being under the fundamental aspect of time; its fundamental method is that of causality, for a causal connection between two phenomena is a necessary connection between two phenomena following one upon the other in time. This, however, is not the only kind of order and objectivization. There is also a realm of objectivization toward the "ought to be" which transcends the determination of time. In the "ought" is implied the concept of direction, and direction contains a relation to infinity which is impossible to conceive except by a consciousness transcending the determination of time. It is not a consciousness aiming at the concretization of an object within the form of time and its limitations, such as the cognition of natural laws governing an object of nature under the aspect of causality, but the ethical consciousness of man conceiving an ideal state in which the idea of the good will be realized, which is a consciousness of infinity transcending time, since the "ought" can be thought of only as approaching realization in infinity.

In addition to the cognitive and ethical objectivizations, there are other kinds of objectivizations in the aesthetic and religious realms, which are grounded in different aspects of human consciousness. Just as the objectivizations in the realm of natural science and in the realm of ethics are determined by corresponding aspects of human consciousness, so is the aesthetic object and the religious experience determined by definite and particular aspects of human consciousness.

The intention of the Critique of Kant is a refutation of Hume's skepticism. But what makes the understanding of the Critique sometimes difficult is the question concerning the relation of the separate Kantian doctrines to the particular problems raised by Hume. Nor is it clearly established which of the Kantian doctrines are central and which are merely peripheral. So, for instance, the question concerning the existence of external objects or of other minds does not seem to occupy a prominent place in the Critique.

Now it seems to me that the principle of the possibility of experience, which is employed by Kant for the deduction of the categories of thought, has a direct bearing on the question concerning the existence of external objects and that of other minds.

Hume's skepticism concerning the existence of external objects is based on his analysis of ordinary common experience. Hume says: almost all mankind, and philosophers themselves, for the greatest part of their lives, i.e., in their ordinary conduct, when they are not engaged in philosophic reflections, believe that the very things they feel and see are external objects existing continually even while we cease to see or feel them. Some philosophers, however, have been led to the rejection of the reality of external objects on the basis of the reflection that what we actually perceive by the senses does not exist except when we perceive it. The assumption that there are external objects existing independently of us which are the cause of our perceptions is not founded in experience, for we have never directly observed such external objects.

A causal connection between the fact of A with the fact of B is possible to establish only on the basis of our observation of their being habitually conjoined together. But we have never observed the existence of external objects apart from their being objects of perception; we are, therefore, not entitled to maintain that they cause us to perceive what we do perceive. Hence it is gratuitous and unfounded to maintain that there are external objects which are the cause of our perception. For that matter, it is also unfounded to maintain that there are other minds perceiving the same as we do when we are observing and experiencing a certain object. This is Hume's position.[1]

Now it seems to me that if we assume as real only that which is directly perceived by our senses, we could not possibly account for experience altogether. One of the necessary conditions making experience possible is the assumed continuity of the existence of the experienced objects, so long as there is no sufficient reason causing the discontinuance of their existence. This is a necessary assumption without which there would be no experience of reality altogether, for otherwise we would have inexplicable changes of the mental states of men, i.e., of the perceptions that come and go without rime or reason.

The same can be said concerning the existence of other minds. The assumption of the reality of other minds is a necessary assumption, for it is an indispensable condition for the possibility of experience. Man is not alone in the world; his experience is bound up with the like experience of other men; social and mental intercourse, and general scientific knowledge, which is the result of the work of many minds, would be impossible without the assumption of the existence of other minds. All the realms of scientific knowledge have been built up by cooperation of many minds. The fact of scientific experience requires the assumption of the existence of other minds, without which scientific experience is unthinkable. Thus, the continuity of the existence of the external things constituting the objects of experience as well as the community of minds constituting the general subject, i.e., general consciousness of experience, are the necessary conditions for the possibility of experience. Herein is grounded the justification of the assumption of the existence of external objects as well as of the existence of other minds.

Kant's principle of the possibility of experience, from which the reality of synthetic propositions a priori is deduced, has been interpreted by prominent Kantians to refer to scientific experience. The point of departure of the Kantian deduction of the categories of thought is the universality and general validity of mathematics and of the laws of Newtonian physics. He assumes this to be a real and undoubtable fact, from which the deduction is made of the categories of thought as necessary principles and indispensable conditions of experience. The legitimacy of the categories of thought is deduced from the principle of the possibility of experience. Since without the assumption of the categories of thought, experience as such would be impossible, the legitimacy of such categories is logically justified and necessary. The fact of mathematical and physical science is the basis for the Kantian deduction. It was therefore pointed out that by the Kantian reference to experience is meant scientific experience, and by the principle of the possibility of experience is meant the possibility of scientific experience. This is Kant's position with reference to the deduction of the categories of thought. But with reference to the problem before us, namely, the question concerning the continuous existence of objects of experience independently of our actually experiencing them, we have to apply the Kantian principle of the possibility of experience in relation to common experience, i.e., to the prescientific experience of everyday life. Furthermore, the scientific experience cannot be considered entirely detached and separated from common experience. Even though science operates with concepts like atoms and motions and energy, etc., which are not present in the consciousness of our common and vulgar experience, scientific experience is not unrelated to common experience, for it strives, after all, to come down from the plane of pure abstractions, as manifested in the scientific concepts, to explain in a more coherent and systematic form the occurrences of everyday experience.

By understanding the Kantian principle of the possibility of experience as referring both to the scientific as well as to the common and vulgar experience of everyday life, we will understand the Kantian refutation of subjective Berkeleian Idealism and the fundamental distinction which obtains between subjective Idealism, on the one hand, and transcendental or critical Idealism, on the other. While the former denies the reality of existing objects of experience, for the *real* is only the subject and its states, the latter maintains the reality of existing objects of experience, not as objects in themselves but as objects of experience.

Hume's skepticism concerning the existence of external objects and the reality of other minds is closely connected with subjective Idealism. Both are rooted in sensualism. Hume's critical analysis of the concept of external objects which led to skepticism maintains only a noncommittal attitude toward the problem of the existence of external objects. That is to say, it does not deny the reality of external objects, it maintains only that we cannot rightfully demonstrate the existence of such entities. Subjective Idealism, however, has drawn the conclusions from sensualism and has arrived at a position maintaining that only the subject and its states are real, thus denying the existence of external entities.

In our own time there is a revival of Hume's skepticism in the Positivistic school of thought. And as a necessary consequence of sensualism and skepticism we have also subjective Idealism, which denies the existence of external objects.

In a paper entitled "Refutation of Realism," Professor Stace has offered a criticism of Moore's Realism. It must, however, be emphasized that Moore's essay, "Refutation of Idealism," is directed only against subjective Idealism. His arguments have no bearing on critical or transcendental Idealism. The same applies to Stace's arguments in favor of Idealism: they are meant only as a defense of subjective Idealism. While Moore attempts to prove the reality of an external world, i.e., the existence of unexperienced entities, the arguments of Stace are directed toward disproving the assumption of the reality of unexperienced objects. According to Moore the external objects exist even when we are not perceiving them, and according to Stace there is no cogent necessity to assume the existence of things when they are not directly perceived by us. For Stace the logically correct position is that "we have no reason whatever to believe that unexperienced entities exist."[2]

Moore and Stace both agree as to the meaning of the terms "Idealism" and "Realism," namely, that Idealism is a position maintaining that only the subject and its states are real, and not the objects as experienced by the senses. Realism, on the other hand, is a position maintaining the reality of external objects, i.e., the existence of unexperienced entities. This is totally different from the meaning of the terms "subject" and "object" in the spirit of critical philosophy. Kant has defined his position as empirical realism and transcendental idealism. Empirical realism implies the existence of an external world. Things do exist even when we are not perceiving them, for otherwise experience would be impossible. The assumption of the continuity of the existence of the external things is a necessary assumption for the possibility, i.e., the actuality, of experience. The fact of experience is taken for granted; it is an undeniable reality. Otherwise we would live in a chaotic world. And those conditions and assumptions which make this fact possible are thus indispensable and necessary assumptions. The assumption of the continuity of the existence of the external things belongs to those indispensable conditions for the possibility and actuality of experience. Herein is grounded their justification. To maintain with Professor Stace that we are sure of the existence of a piece of paper so long as we are observing and experiencing it, but that we have no right to assert the cntinuance of its existence when we turn away from it, is to negate the very reality of experience.

On the other hand, the very meaning of the term "existence" should be defined as existence of things for a subject constituted in a definite manner. There are no things in themselves, as objects of cognition, apart from their relation to human consciousness. Consequently, the existence of external objects means existence in relation to human consciousness.

Even when we are not directly perceiving the objects, we are aware of their continuing existence in a definite manner generally common to man, for otherwise there would be no experience altogether. This is empirical realism. But things do not exist apart from their relation to human consciousness. We have no justification for asserting the reality of things in themselves, i.e., things abstracted from their relation to human thought and consciousness, for we are in possession of no possible method by which the *noumenal* world of things existing in themselves could be approached. The human mind is always employing forms of thought in its perception and the conception of objects, for the subject cannot depart radically at any given moment from his frame of reference.

The term "subject" here is not to be understood as the psychological individual subject, but as the human subject in general. Since the external objects exist as possible objects of cognition only in relation to human consciousness, it is transcendental idealism. Transcendental is not identical with transcendent, but is rather its opposite, according to the Kantian definition of the terms. Under "transcendental" is to be understood the ultimate forms of thought constitutive to human consciousness and necessary for the cognition of any object, while "transcendent" refers to entities existing in themselves and apart from their relation to the constitutive forms of thought and consciousness necessary for the cognition of objects.

The conception of empirical realism of critical philosophy is fundamentally different from the realism of Moore and his school. According to the position of the latter, the objects of experience exist apart from any relation to forms of thought and consciousness, that is to say, they exist as things in themselves. According to the former, objects of experience exist even when we are not experiencing them, but they exist only as objects of possible experience by the human mind and in relation to human consciousness. But they do not exist as things in themselves and abstracted from all possible relation to human consciousness.

Likewise, transcendental idealism is fundamentally different from the subjective idealism of Stace. According to the latter, only the subject and its states are real, nothing beyond it. We are sure of the existence of an object, so long as we are observing and experiencing it. But we have no right to assert the continuance of its existence while we are not experiencing it. According to transcendental idealism, however, objects of experience do exist as such, even while we are not experiencing them. But they exist as *possible* objects of experience by a human consciousness, not as things in themselves. Existence as such is a term which cannot be defined otherwise than in relation to the forms of thought constitutive to human consciousness.

I am certain of the continuous existence of the table upon which I am writing, even after I have left the room. But the assertion of its continuous existence at the same place does not imply the reality of the table as a thing in itself. The thing in itself is beyond the limits of possible comprehension. We are not entitled to assume the reality of a thing which is beyond all possible comprehension. The certainty of the continuous existence of the table independent of, and separated from, the perceiving subject is confined to the table as a phenomenon, i.e., as a sensuous object given to a possible comprehension by a subject constituted in a definite manner and endowed with certain forms of sensibility and understanding. This follows conclusively from the Kantian doctrine of time and space as forms of sensibility, i.e., as forms necessarily connected with the subject.

A mathematical object, such as a triangle or a circle, is an ideational object; it is not connected with the forms of time and space. A triangle or a circle does not exist here or there; nor can it be stated of such an object that it exists now and then. However, the table as an object of possible perception is not an object of thought but a phenomenon, and not a thing in itself. A phenomenal object perceived at a certain time and at a definite place continues its existence as such even when I do not directly perceive it, so long as there are no causes affecting its destruction or its change of place.

Subjective or empirical idealism denies the reality of external objects; it maintains that every object is nothing else but a bundle of perceptions. Accordingly, our experience of objects through the sense-data is to be compared to a dream. We can speak with certainty only of our subjective experiences but not of an objective reality. The presentations of the objects cannot be coherently connected with one another, nor can they be brought into an ordered experience valid for any subject. According to such a view, the reality of scientific experience which tries to establish law and order among the phenomena is difficult to vindicate.

Critical or transcendental idealism in the Kantian sense of the term considers time and space as necessary forms of sensibility, i.e., a priori given intuitions. The objects given in these forms are objective phenomena for all subjects, equally constituted and endowed with the necessary forms of sensibility. The phenomena are real objects, inasmuch as they are determinable by synthetic a priori forms. Since, however, time and space are forms of sensibility, the objects perceived could never be things in themselves. All our objects of experience are necessarily tied up with the forms of time and space. Hence, cognitions by these forms could comprehend phenomena but not things in themselves.

Thus, when Bertrand Russell says, "Belief in the existence of things outside my own biography must, from the standpoint of theoretical logic, be regarded as a prejudice, not as a well-grounded theory,"[3] he again sets in opposition to one another "my own biography" and "the existence of things outside" it, as if they were two separate, independent, and self-sustaining entities. The truth is, however, that "my own biography" (i.e., the subject) is unthinkable without a relation to things outside it. Nor could the "existence of things outside" the subject be defined without any relation to human thought and consciousness constituted in a definite manner. The very meaning of the term "existence" implies existence of things for a mind with its indispensable forms of thought and cognition.

Lovejoy argues that the existence of things during the interperceptual intervals can be inferred from the law of causation.[4] He says: "The same uniform causal sequences observed within experience appear to go on in the same manner when not experienced. You build a fire in your grate of a certain quantity of coal, of a certain chemical composition. Whenever you remain in the room, there occurs a typical succession of sensible phenomena according to an approximately regular schedule of clock-time; in, say, half an hour the coal is half consumed; at the end of the hour the grate contains only ashes. If you build a fire of the same quantity of the same material under the same conditions, leave the room, and return after any given time has elapsed, you get approximately the same sense-experience as you would have had at the corresponding moment if you had remained in the room. You infer, therefore, that the fire has been burning as usual during your absence, and that being perceived is not a condition necessary for the occurrence of the process."

Lovejoy assumes thus the reality of the law of causation from which he infers the existence of unexperienced objects. But when one considers as real only what is immediately given to our senses and doubts the existence of the objects during the interperceptual intervals, he will be consistent in doubting also the reality of the law of causation. The latter is no more certain than the former. It is, therefore, illegitimate to take the law of causation for granted and to infer from it the existence of unexperienced things. Moreover, the Positivist, for whom reality is grounded in the "given" perceptions, who is, therefore, skeptical concerning the existence of objects during the interperceptual intervals, must necessarily be skeptical concerning the law of causation even in relation to observed and experienced objects simply because causation can never be given through perceptions. Through perceptions we experience the succession of phenomena one upon the other, but not the causal connection between them. There is thus more reason for skepticism with regard to the reality of the law of causation than with reference to the existence of unexperienced objects. The former cannot therefore be posited as a basic assumption for the purpose of deducing the existence of the latter.

Now Professor Stace writes with reference to Lovejoy's argument: "This argument is simply a *petitio principii*. It assumes that we must believe that the law of causality continues to operate in the universe when no one is observing it. But the law of causality is, it is clear, one aspect of the universe, the unobserved existence of which is the very thing to be proved. Why must we believe that causation continues to operate during interperceptual intervals? Obviously, the case as regards unexperienced processes and laws is in exactly the same position as the case regarding unexperienced things."[5] Stace admits the reality of the law of causality in relation to observed and experienced objects, he doubts its reality only in relation to unobserved and unexperienced objects, i.e., its operation during the interperceptual intervals. "Just as we cannot perceive unexperienced things, so we cannot perceive unexperienced processes and laws. Just as we cannot infer from anything which we experience the existence of unexperienced things, so we cannot infer from anything we experience the existence of unexperienced processes and laws."[6] But the very meaning of the law of causality is the determination of a necessary connection between two phenomena A and B, i.e., when A is given, B must necessarily follow. Consequently, when one grants the possibility of observing causality, that is to say, the establishment of a necessary connection between two phenomena on the basis of experience and observation, there is no need for always observing the succession of one upon the other. Since the connection between the phenomena is already established, when one is given the other must necessarily follow. It is incongruous to admit, on the one hand, the reality of the law of causality in relation to two experienced phenomena A and B, and to doubt, on the other hand, the effect of A upon B when the latter is not directly observed and experienced. It is a contradiction in terms to grant the law of causation on the basis of perception and sensuous experience and to be skeptical with reference to the effect of the cause when the former is not directly perceived and experienced.

The objection to Lovejoy's arguments should rather be based on the consideration that skepticism concerning the existence of unexperienced objects must necessarily lead to skepticism concerning the very reality of the law of causality even in relation to observed and experienced objects. Skepticism with regard to the existence of unexperienced objects is grounded in the position that only what is immediately and directly given to us through the sense-data is real, and the unobserved and unexperienced objects are not directly perceived by us. Such a position must consistently and necessarily imply a skepticism with regard to the reality of the law of causation as such, since the causal connection between two phenomena is never directly "given" to us through sense perceptions.

If we assume as real only what is directly and immediately "given" to our senses and are accordingly skeptical about the existence of objects while we are not perceiving them, we have no right to assume the reality of the law of causality, in order to deduce from it the existence of interperceptual objects. Neither of them can be derived from the other, for each is equally subject to doubt on the basis of an extreme sensualism. Lovejoy's argument attempting to derive the existence of unexperienced things from the law of causation, as if the latter were more certain than the former, is thus untenable and self-contradictory.

The position of critical philosophy, however, is that the law of causality is a necessary concept grounded in the principle of the possibility of experience. Since without the assumption of the concept of causality, there would be no experience altogether, it is a necessary concept demanded by the very fact of experience. On the basis of the same principle, we derive the necessity of the existence of objects as possible objects of experience, i.e., as phenomena, for without the assumption of the existence of objects independent of our observing and experiencing them, the very fact of experience would have to be denied. Thus, both assumptions, namely, that of the reality of the law of causality, and that of the existence of unexperienced phenomena, as possible objects of experience, independent of our actual and immediate experience, as well as the existence of other minds, are derived from one and the same principle, namely, the possibility of experience. They both equally need a justification and legitimization, which can be derived from the Kantian principle of possibility of experience.

NOTES

1. Cf. G. E. Moore, "Hume's Philosophy," in *Readings in Philosophical Analysis* (New York, 1949), pp. 351 ff.
2. *Readings in Philosophical Analysis*, p. 372.
3. *Analysis of Mind*, p. 133.
4. *The Revolt Against Dualism*, p. 268.
5. Stace, "The Refutation of Realism," in *Readings in Philosophical Analysis*, p. 369.
6. Ibid.

RELIGION AND THE ARTS

BERNARD J. BAMBERGER

THERE has been a marked upswing of interest in the arts among religious leaders. We no longer build tired Gothic churches or synthetic "Moorish" synagogues; there is now a great variety of styles, and at times new concepts of the purpose and function of religious structures have emerged. Architects and theologians have met in conferences to clarify norms of ecclesiastical architecture. Much new and unconventional music has been composed for worship, often on commission; rock music has been utilized for liturgical purposes, and experiments have been made in multi-media services. Synagogues and churches, moreover, have been supporting artistic endeavor as such: the concerts, art shows, and dramatic performances they have sponsored are not always limited to explicitly religious themes.

All this is excellent and desirable. The artistic community and the religious community have much to give each other. But they are not, as they once were, one community. This increased cooperation, in fact, underscores a number of problems. The practical issues that arise when a religious institution deals with an artist—what kind of decoration is appropriate for a church, for example, or what kind of music is suitable for worship—do not lend themselves readily to generalization. Obviously an avant-garde artist will not have the same outlook as a middle-class congregation that can afford to employ him. But the possible disagreements can probably be worked out better in practice than in theory.

But there are broad themes that require our examination. Here we shall inquire: Since both religion and the arts are concerned with "spiritual" matters, is there any basic difference between them, and in what does such a difference consist? Is there validity to the assertion that worship is akin to poetry—a notion not infrequently heard from liberal pulpits?[1] Such a theme, I trust is proper for an essay intended to honor my friend Levi A. Olan, who through so many years has labored for a Jewish theology that shall be both affirmative and reasonable. (And he has a touch of the artist too; did he not play the fiddle in earlier days?)

I

In the classical world, poets were often characterized as inspired seers; the other arts, however, were treated as highly skilled crafts, which were not sources of supernal vision. The concept of the poet as visionary seems to have disappeared with the classic civilization of which it was a part. In the Middle Ages, all the religious arts were subject to strict ecclesiastical control, while secular artistic productions had to please the patron who footed the bill. This situation lasted through the eighteenth century.

But with the rise of romanticism, the image of the artist as seer was reborn and much enlarged. The artist was glorified as autonomous creator, the bearer of a message, a free spirit subject to no control but that of his own inspiration. Beethoven saw himself as charged with a mission to all mankind. Shelley and Hugo claimed oracular authority for the poet—in the first instance, for themselves. And for decades Goethe ruled as a potentate of the spirit (though his realm included not only poetry, but science and philosophy as well).

This notion of the artist as seer has survived the romantic epoch. Mondrian insisted that his painting had metaphysical implications. Penderecki and Beckett are thought to "speak to our condition." Theologians today expound not only the scriptures and traditions of their several communities, but also the novels of Dostoyevski and Camus, the poetry of Eliot, the theater of the absurd, and even the canvases of Jackson Pollack.

This could mean simply that the theologians recognize contemporary sources of revelation, which supplement the old sources without necessarily contradicting or superseding them. Another approach, however, is represented by Schopenhauer. The latter advocated the contemplation of beauty—especially listening to music—as an anodyne for the suffering imposed on us by a radically evil existence. Art was to be a refuge for a generation which no longer possessed faith. And beyond doubt, today many people who do not engage in personal prayer or public worship seek spiritual refreshment and renewal by going to concerts or listening to records, looking at paintings, or reading literary classics.

Does it make any difference by which door we enter the realm of the spirit?

II

The answer is that in certain ways art is more like science than it is like religion.

Science is autonomous. It is founded on rules of method which must be followed meticulously in investigating and explaining natural phenomena. Strict adherence to these rules is the only *value* which science affirms. Science as such knows no good or bad, but only the scientifically valid or the reverse. The discoveries of science may be applied to beneficent or destructive ends; and within scientific thought there is no norm for distinguishing useful from harmful ends, and no reason to choose one more than another. Nor is the validity of a scientific hypothesis impaired in the slightest by the immoral or anti-social character of the person who proposes it. He may be a brute, a traitor, or a heroin dealer; but if his theory is confirmed by experimental evidence, it is sound. And a saintly character is no guarantee of scientific excellence.

The arts, too, have become essentially autonomous. A work of art has to be judged by artistic norms. The latter, admittedly, are not as clear, objective, and unequivocal as those of scientific method. The element of personal taste cannot be avoided, and critical consensus is subject to change with the passing of time. But changing fashions in the arts result from changes in aesthetic standards. Artistic merit is largely independent of moral and social considerations, except of course in totalitarian lands. Baudelaire may not be a guide to virtue, but he wrote better poetry than the estimable and amiable Longfellow. Wagner was a monster of egoism, ingratitude, and treachery— to say nothing of his anti-Semitism—but the magnitude of his musical achievement is undeniable. Indeed, it would be hard to find music that expresses as much kindliness and compassion as *Die Meistersinger*—though the composer was utterly lacking in those qualities.

Of course, a great work of art may also be the vehicle of constructive ethical and social teaching. The Book of Amos and Beethoven's *Fidelio* may serve as familiar instances. The burning poetry of the one and the sublime music of the other enhance the impact of their message, and their lofty intent consecrates the art. But their artistic merits are not determined by the soundness of their ethical teachings. One can find noble sentiments galore in inferior books and plays, and some extraordinary works of art are morally neutral or even nihilistic.

III

At this point we see a plain difference between the arts (and science) and biblical religion. The most eloquent and compelling sermon loses its cogency for us if we know, or think, that the preacher's life does not square with his professions. Many persons have been repelled by organized religion because they found its proponents to be morally deficient or socially insensitive. I think that those on the outside or on the fringes of the churches have sometimes been unreasonable and intolerant. The adherents of any religion, being human, will have their share of human frailties. Nevertheless, the critics and dissenters are right in expecting avowedly religious people to exemplify in marked degree those moral qualities which religion inculcates.

Thus far we have been comparing the creative artist with the representative of religion. But the contrast is at least as striking when we consider the arts and religion from the standpoint of the average "consumer."

Schopenhauer's use of music as an escape from the tragedy of life is not essentially different from the use of alcohol and marijuana for the same purpose, even though it may be more refined and less risky. Now religion is often utilized for a similar end. People frankly come to public worship in search of calm, relief from tension, and hope in the midst of stress. There is a recognizable parallel between the taut and restless person who tries to get to sleep by repeating the Twenty-third Pslam and the insomniac nobleman for whose relief Bach composed the *Goldberg Variations*.

Religion and art can also provide a different kind of experience—the experience of emotional excitement and exaltation. The Christian revival meeting, the whirling of dervishes, and the Hasidic dance are obvious examples. Earlier religions employed more brutal and shocking means, and even the more conventional religious communities have moments that stir the blood. It goes without saying that similar effects can be generated by artistic means. Tension is an essential element in most drama; music and dance can rouse participants and spectators alike to a high pitch of excitement, and are often utilized for this purpose in a religious context.

This phenomenon merits fuller scrutiny than can be given here. Apparently human beings feel that existence is enhanced, that life acquires immediate meaning, in any situation that stimulates the flow of adrenalin. No one is bored or disillusioned when in military combat, or struggling with hurricane or shipwreck, or straining to scale a precipice. This no doubt explains why some individuals court physical danger and others gamble for sums they cannot afford. The artistic and religious experiences described above are a safer, partly vicarious means of achieving the thrills that at least for the moment add a sense of meaningfulness to our personal lives.

There is nothing inherently wrong in the desire for periods of calm reassurance or the desire for moments of exaltation and enthusiasm. Both are normal and proper, and all the historic religions provide some response to these needs.

But biblical religion—and Judaism most of all—adds another indispensable ingredient. Judaism is not only experience, but also commitment. The artistic experience, whether it is relaxing or exciting, is just experience; it implies no subsequent demands. Perhaps that is one of its attractions to our contemporaries. But religion, as understood in the Jewish tradition, is not just the blissful practice of the presence of God. It is discipline of commandments, directed largely to our relations with other individuals and our participation in the labors of the community. The most sublime emotion is wasted unless it finds expression in righteous deeds.

This is not to derogate the arts or to minimize their importance. The preceding discussion has not taken account of other values in the artistic experience: intellectual stimulation, the broadening of horizons, and sheer enjoyment. It would be ungrateful to overlook all this largesse. But whatever else they are, the concert hall and the art collection are not religious sanctuaries or surrogates for religious sanctuaries. The concert hall and museum offer us much; we accept what we can or what we choose, and then go our way. The religious sanctuary offers much and it demands much. That is the irreducible difference.

IV

Liberal religious thinkers have repeatedly suggested an analogy between poetry and worship. To examine such a notion intelligently, we must first state what we mean by poetry. Obviously the difference between poetry and prose is not just a matter of meter and rhyme. In my opinion, the difference can be stated as follows: In prose, the words convey (or should convey) a single well-defined meaning, no more, no less. But poetry implies or suggests more than the words themselves plainly mean. However this plus is achieved—by rhythm, melody, metaphor, understatement, or some other device—we sense an added something that vibrates around the construable meaning of the words.

Now the language of worship, by its very nature, has to be allusive. God cannot be described, still less defined, by human minds and human tongues. Whatever we say in prayer is inadequate. But language that somehow suggests the mystery and wonder of existence, and the grandeur and love of the God to Whom we reach out, is less inadequate than the precise prose of everyday affairs. I am convinced that with all the good intentions and philosophic skill at our command, we cannot escape anthropomorphism when we think and speak about or to God. I can agree fully with the statement that worship is akin to poetry, if it means that our prayers and aspirations attempt to relate us to a Reality far beyond our power to envision clearly, and that we employ metaphor and allusion to reduce a little the gap between us and our God.

But I am troubled by the suspicion that those who equate poetry and worship have something else in mind. Instead of seeing in liturgy the means of extending, if only by a trifle, the ladder that stretches from earth toward heaven, they may regard worship as something completely earthbound. Contemporary worship seems to be viewed as a kind of artistic experience designed to awaken in us the kind of emotions felt by our forebears who really believed in a living God. Much of the current popularity of Hasidism in liberal Jewish circles seems to express this intent; it is a kind of theatrical performance, a calculated attempt to evoke the mood of Hasidic worship without the foundation of unquestioning belief that made the mood possible and genuine. One thinks of a Hebrew proverb (the source is not known to me, but it is definitely not in the Talmud): *Metav shir k'zavo,* which may be tactfully translated, "The charm of poetry is its depiction of the imaginary."

Such an approach seems to me a counsel of desperation. Perhaps there is no alternative for those who want to preserve the positive values inherent in synagogue life, but are unable with honesty to make a positive theistic affirmation. With all respect for their sincerity, one may doubt that such an approach will work. I find myself much in sympathy with a recent writer on a related topic, who concluded his article with the words, "Let us pray—to Some One Else, if you please . . ."[2]

NOTES

This essay (with slight changes) is to appear as a chapter of a book to be published by Behrman House and tentatively entitled *The Style of Jewish Theology*.

1. For several generations, liberal theologians have treated prophetic revelation as analogous to artistic and poetic inspiration. Perhaps it is time for us to rethink that notion carefully; I have not tried to do so here because for the present I have no more to offer than a sense of uneasiness on the subject.
2. Edward Graham, "Winds of Liturgical Reform," *Judaism*, Winter 1974.

MAN, GOD, AND HISTORY:
A Study in Origins

JACK BEMPORAD

Ideal and Actual

In the first chapter of his great work *Mimesis,* Auerbach contrasts the characterization of biblical figures and events with those of Homer. It is a very instructive comparison for an understanding of the biblical world view. A brief summary of Auerbach will enlighten us in these matters.

Auerbach tells us of an ancient incident in the *Odyssey* which occurred after Odysseus returned home. It happens at perhaps the most crucial time of the entire narrative. Odysseus comes home in disguise, hoping to gain the upper hand over Penelope's suitors by keeping his identity a secret. However, Euryclea, who was his nursemaid, discovers him because she recognizes the scar, which she accidentally touches while, in accordance with the custom of dealing with guests, she washes his feet. This is an extremely dramatic moment since the whole plan of his return may be upset if he is discovered. At this tense and important juncture, Homer begins to describe the scar, how Odysseus received it on a boar hunt with his grandfather. And after a few lines one forgets that Odysseus has just returned home and is in imminent danger. One is entranced by the boar hunt and the events concerning it. Homer is a bewitching storyteller. He delights the senses. Nothing remains hidden.

Every event is minutely and precisely described, what the people are wearing, where they come from, and what they are doing. Everything is external; it has its place, its history, and is always on the surface. If we were to characterize Homer's style and character, we would say that it was (1) externalized, nothing is in the background, everything is in the foreground, and (2) static, there is no development of character. Auerbach states that "Odysseus on his return is exactly the same as he was when he left Ithaca two decades earlier."[1] There is no growth or change in the depth of his character. He merely passes from one state to another.

How different is the atmosphere and the dimension of the Bible! Here, to contrast it with Homer's story, Auerbach tells the story of the binding of Isaac. Abraham is called, and he responds, "Here am I." He is not described at a particular place or time. God has made a demand on Abraham, and Abraham is ready to respond to that demand. All the items mentioned—the ass, the lads, the knife, and the wood—are the bare elements of the drama. They are all ingredients in the future demand that will be made. The present scene is dominated by the demand made by God and the response of Abraham. It is tension and suspense that sets the tone of the story. It is not just the existence of Isaac which is in question, but the existence of Israel and the realization of the promise made by God to Abraham that through him and his seed all of the families of the earth will be blessed.[2] The contrast between Homer and the Bible emphasizes that element of juxtaposition betwen demand and response, between ideal and actual, which is characteristic of the biblical world view. The very fact that all the elements described are ingredients of the future event, so that they all find their place in terms of the demand, tends to indicate that the descriptive features are dominated by the overtones and dimensions of the values involved. Auerbach gives voice to this when he states that "the two realms of the sublime and the everyday are not only actually unseparated but basically inseparable."[3] Auerbach seeks to demonstrate that the polarity of demand and response is characteristic of the very style of the Bible.

Auerbach maintains that "the human beings in the Biblical stories have greater depths of time, fate and consciousness than do the human beings in Homer. . . . they are not so entirely immersed in its present that they do not remain continually conscious of what has happened to them earlier and elsewhere . . . Abraham's actions are explained not only by what is happening to him at the moment nor yet only by his character (as Achilles' action by his courage and his pride, and Odysseus' by his versatility and foresightedness), but by his previous history, he remembers, he is constantly conscious of what God has promised him and what God has already accomplished for him—his soul is torn between desperate rebellion and hopeful expectation; his silent obedience is multilayered, has background. Such a problematic psychological situation as this is impossible for any of the Homeric heroes, whose destiny is clearly defined and who wake every morning as if it were the first day of their lives."[4]

This element of past and future, of memory and expectation, and its intrinsic connection to the multilayered transformations that take place in the biblical figures, illustrates the historical character of man in the Bible. Past and future are intertwined with individual, national, and finally universal hopes, and result in individual, national, and finally universal transformations. The Bible sees all events as fitting into the structure of universal history. As Auerbach points out, "The Old Testament . . . presents universal history; it begins with the beginning of time, with the creation of the world, and will end with the last days with the fulfilling of the convenant. . . . everything else that happens in the world can only be conceived as an element in this sequence." Each of the great figures of the Old Testament, from Adam to the prophets, embodies a moment of this vertical connection. God chose and formed these men to the end of embodying His essence and will—yet choice and formation do not coincide, for the latter proceeds gradually, historically, during the earthly life of him upon whom the choice has fallen. How the process is accomplished, what terrible trials such a formation inflicts, can be seen from our story of Abraham's sacrifice. Herein lies the reason why the great figures of the Old Testament are so much more fully developed, so much more fraught with their own biographical past, so much more distinct as individuals, than are the Homeric heroes.[5]

Biblical history is bound up with the transformation of character in the Bible. We have shown that in Homer, Odysseus is unchanged by the events that happen in his life; and how completely different this is in the Bible. This is well illustrated in the story of the Patriarch Jacob. Jacob was a deceiver. He deceived both Esau and Isaac. He stole both the birthright and the blessing. However, Jacob the deceiver was himself to be deceived. He was deceived by Laban when the wife given him was Leah instead of the expected Rachel. He was deceived by his children when they told him Joseph was dead. He lost his beloved wife, Rachel. His life was a tragic one.[6] Through the different events of his life Jacob changes. He gains depth. There is a pathos in Jacob's later life. The symbolic transformation of Jacob in his struggle with the angel is the key to his transformation. His life is still tragic, but he shall no more be called Jacob but Israel. The transformation of Jacob to Israel sets the stage for the later transformation of the descendants of Jacob into the people Israel by Moses, and then the prophetic transformation of a national entity into a people with a mission for all mankind. It is against the background of this universal historic dimension that each biblical leader is defined in terms of a task to be accomplished, a good to be realized. The character of the task is such as to transcend any one individual's attempt. Moses was faced with the demand to rescue his people. To transform the multitudes of men and women and children into one nation. He was the liberator, the lawgiver, the greatest prophet, and yet he never reaches the land of Canaan. Amos is told to prophesy against the land of Israel. He pleads and implores the people to repent, and he, too, fails. All the prophets were failures, none actualized the demand made upon them. Their task was an infinite task. Their goal was an infinite one, and yet the demand was still there. The rabbinic dictum, "It is not yours to finish the task, but neither is it yours to exempt yourself from it," is an incisive summary of the prophetic pathos.

This idea that one should fulfill the demand in spite of its outcome, that even if one were to fail, still one must attempt it, can be seen most clearly in the consecration vision of Isaiah.[7] Isaiah is in the Temple. He is overwhelmed by a feeling of holiness. He conceives of God as perfectly Holy and becomes aware of his own imperfection, of his own finiteness. He is a man of unclean lips in a nation of unclean lips. The demand comes forth—whom shall we send? who shall go for us? The response. Send me. Once he takes the task upon himself, the realization comes upon him that he will and must fail. He is told to make the people hear; but they will not hear. He must make the people see; but they will not see. He must make them understand; but they will not understand. He will not succeed. He knows this before he starts. Yet he must strive to answer the demand. He must fulfill the obligation. Isaiah warns the people to repent or beware of the doom that will ensue. They do not repent, and it seems that doom is imminent because Sennacherib is at their doors. But some unseen event forces Sennacherib to retreat and the people are saved. The people shout with joy. Isaiah weeps because the people do not understand that their salvation must be a moral one. They do not realize that peace can only come about through their actualization of the ideal. It is their treatment of one another which brings about real disaster, the disaster of injustice and inhumanity, and only if they repent and change will they be worthy of having peace.[8] This demand, which is accepted though unrealizable, presents at once the essence and pathos of the dichotomy between ideal and actual—this is the pathos of the Bible.

Several basic elements become apparent once we understand the biblical concept of man as being shaped by an ideal goal—a demand—an imperative to action. Time becomes an anticipation. The future goal hovers over and shapes the present. It was Hermann Cohen who most clearly saw this transformation of time in the Bible. "Time," he states, "becomes future and only future. Past and present are submerged in this time of the future. This return to time is the purest idealization. Before this idea all existence vanishes. The existence of man is transcended in his future being. . . . the prophets are the idealists of history, their seerdom created the concept of history as the being of the future." Cassirer summarizes Cohen's view by stating that "for the prophetic consciousness the whole of cosmic, astronomical time disappears along with nature; in its place arises a new intuition of time which has reference solely to the history of mankind. Moreover, this history is not seen as past history but as a religious history of the future."[9]

The second element that appears is that the goal which constitutes the demand or the imperative to action is not a finite goal, but a universal, historic one.[10] The fact that each one of the biblical leaders does not succeed implies that one cannot realize the goal in one's lifetime or even in the span of a nation's life. The ideal of the peoplehood of Israel is indissolubly bound up with mankind, and hence the goal becomes constantly broadened. Man, in his continual striving to actualize an infinite goal, continually accomplishes finite tasks. The goal is infinite but the realization is finite. It is this dichotomy between the infinite task and the finite achievement which brings the moral question to the fore.

It is not the success or failure of the task that is important; it is the principle of action that is important. Isaiah knew that he would not succeed even before he started.[11] Yet this did not prevent him from exerting all his power to bring about the actualization of the ideal. Jeremiah was jailed, left in a pit to die, almost executed. Yet this did not deter him from his imperative. Perhaps the most dramatic moment in prophetic literature is represented in Jeremiah's trial, where the priests and prophets were intent on killing him. He did not try to save his life. Nor did he retract one iota of what he had said. He said that "of a truth the Lord had sent me, do with me what you will, but know that you are taking innocent blood."[12] Biblical ethics is not concerned with the results but with the principles of action. It is in this sense that the idea of an infinite task and its concomitant finite achievement is asserted in the character of the categorical imperative. [13] The Bible sees the ethical dimension as the a priori that gives man's task reality and without which man would lose his historical basis.

These elements in the development of the biblical idea of man and history are only possible within the context of a specific kind of God concept. Before we can deal more specifically with the meaning of man and history, we must make the biblical God concept explicit.

The Idea of God as Transcendence and His Relationship to Man

The prophets view God as unique, transcendent, and morally related to man. Such a view is in opposition to all ancient religions. In all ancient religions the two central ideas are that of individual soul and its fate. The gods are the forces of nature, which must be coerced or propitiated for the attainment of terrestrial happiness or immortality. In these mythological views, the business of the god is to help men conquer other men, or to help man against the inimical power of the universe. In such a view there is an attempt to appease nature. The appeasement of nature or the gods becomes the purpose of religion. Hand in hand, then, with the idea of the gods as natural forces is the task of mythical religion to appease, bribe, and manipulate these forces through sacrifice and prayer.

The essence of prophetic religion is the rejection of the mythical. [14] It does away with the gods in nature and therefore brings about a transformation in man's relationship to God. Prophetic religion arises with the idea that man's relationship to God is moral in character. God makes a moral demand on man. He is seen as pure spirit, separate from the natural world. No images or representations of God are possible. As long as the gods are forces of nature (gods of fertility, rain, harvesting, etc.), worship will be aimed at appeasing these natural forces. Since man's needs are many, the gods are many. But when God is seen as beyond nature, then man's relation to God is not one of appeasement but one of ethical obligation. Perhaps the most explicit statement of this opposition occurs in the Book of Micah. The year is 701 B.C.E.,[15] the situation drastic: Jerusalem is surrounded, doom is imminent. The people are confused. They do not know what to do. How shall one manipulate God to avoid the calamity? How shall one appease or influence God? Shall one come before God, "with burnt offerings, with calves of a year old? Will the Lord be pleased with thousands of rams with ten thousand rivers of oil?" Shall one give his firstborn for his transgression, the fruit of his body—will the sacrifice of children appease God's anger? Micah's answer echoes down through the centuries: "It hath been told thee, O man, what is good and what the Lord doth require of thee. But to do justly, to love mercy, and to walk humbly with thy God."[16] The preexilic prophets fought against sacrifice, pleading that God wants justice and righteousness.[17] God makes a demand of man announcing the imperative for his action.

When God is seen as transcendent, as beyond nature, then man's relation to God can be a spiritual one. God is set over against nature; only He has true being. This is described poetically in the Second Isaiah. There it is said, "To whom, then, will ye liken God, or what likeness will you compare to Him? . . . Behold the nations are as a drop of a bucket and are counted as the small dust of the balances."[18] God is transcendent. He is unique. Yet He stands in relation to man, invoking the imperative to action. The contrast between God as a force in nature and God as a transcendent spiritual being is clearly illustrated by an incident in Elijah's life. Elijah was confronted by a shattering wind, and then an earthquake, and after that a fire. But God was not in any of these. God is not a force of nature. After these forces was a still, small voice. The still, small voice, the imperative to action, was Elijah's communication with God.[19]

Once God is seen as a transcendent, unique, spiritual being, then the concepts of man and nature become fundamentally different. First of all, the unity and transcendence of God gives rise to the concept of man as transcending nature. Man is not only a natural but a spiritual being. This can be seen in the creation story. God creates man as a "thou" having a special place in the universe. Eichrodt described the difference between man and nature rightly when he states, ''Man is not simply a piece of nature . . . the earlier account of the creation ascribes the clear boundary between man and the animals which prevents man from finding his complement and completion in the subhuman creation, to the effects of man's independent spiritual nature, by which he is set on God's side. In man's destiny as being made in the image of God, the priestly thinker however brings together the sayings about man's special place in the creation and gives pregnant utterance to the thought that man cannot be submerged in nature or merged in the laws of the cosmos, as long as he remains true to his destiny. The creator's greatest gift to man, that of the personal I, necessarily places him in analogy with God's being at a distance from nature.''[20] It is important to note further that this special dignity that God gives man is universal. There is no distinction between men, between slave and free, citizen and foreigner. The idea of man in the Bible is man as mankind. The historic goal is one for all of mankind and not for Israel alone. Only a universal God could establish a universal goal for all men and all nations. Therefore, the transcendence of God made the idea of the unity of man and history possible. The unity and transcendence of God gave rise to the transcendent goal, an ought which transcended nature since it was moral in essence.

The concept of nature was likewise transformed with the idea of the unity and transcendence of God. Nature was no more full of gods. It became possible to act meaningfully in nature since there were no more forces to be appeased. Instead of propitiating nature, it was now man's task to transform nature. This is a crucial point. As long as man was tied to nature in such a way that nature dominated man's life, man could only attempt to bribe nature, to appease her powers. Once nature was seen as devoid of the gods, then it became possible to transform nature. Man no more sought to propitiate nature but to transform it. This made moral action possible. It likewise made science possible.[21] As long as nature was full of gods, then it could never be understood. It could never be consistently apprehended, since it was seen as the result of a number of separate powers. But with the concept of God as a transcendent creator and of the universe as His creation, the idea of cosmos became possible. The world became the matrix of creation, the arena in which one acted to actualize the ideal. Only in a world where there is a unitary source for all being could moral responsibility be possible. Man realized that he had the power to act and transform the universe. He realized that he was not helpless before it. Man, aware of his spiritual being and his spiritual relation to God, sought to actualize an ideal goal that transcended nature.

We have seen that the concept of God as a unique, transcendent, spiritual being made it possible for man to overcome the tyranny of nature and see it in such a manner that it became no more an object of propitiation or appeasement but of transformation. We have also seen that only such a concept of God could make possible the idea of man as a spiritual being transcending nature in his own right, and having an idea of what ought to be. The spiritual character of God transformed the whole relationship between God and man. Man became related to God in an ethical, spiritual way. God demanded justice and righteousness. Man responded to that demand by striving to achieve the goal demanded of him. In striving to transform nature, morality became the rule of his life.

The Idea of Man and History

The biblical idea of history is dominated by a goal which the historical process is to actualize. That goal is the Messianic Age. The Messianic Age is essentially social in the sense that all events are measured in terms of a just society where "nation shall not lift up sword against nation, neither shall they learn war anymore; but they shall sit every man under his vine and fig tree and none shall make them afraid."[22] The prophets pictured the Messianic Age as the goal of man's historical and social striving. In this society equality shall reign, oppression and exploitation shall cease, and justice will be executed throughout the world. The world will be a world of peace. The Messianic vision in the Bible pictures for us a utopian society of peace and brotherhood. Now, one of the most significant characteristics of this social utopia is that it is interconnected with the historical process. It is not a utopia which is metaphysically beyond history with no effect on the historical process. Rather, it is the only way that a historical process is possible. The Messianic Age is the ideal goal that shapes and defines the historical process and man's action within history.

In the construction of events in time and space in terms of a goal which ought to be realized, the Bible subordinated the cosmological element, which is the only element of change in ancient religions, to the historical character of change. In this respect the cosmological character of natural events and cycles is wholly transformed to fit into the context of the historical process. Nature and natural process became subject to historical demands.

The biblical idea of the Messianic Age envisioned the complete historical transformation of nature so that it would be completely fused and dominated by the moral idea. In this manner there could no longer be any foundation for cosmological religion. Cassirer expresses this clearly when he states, "Just as a new heart is required of man, so there must also be a 'new heaven and a new earth'—a natural sub-stratum as it were of the new spirit in which all time and change are seen."

The poetic imagery of this new order is vividly described as one where nature's antagonisms are overcome, where the wolf shall dwell with the lamb and the leopard with the kid, where the lion shall eat straw like an ox and the knowledge of God fill the earth.[23]

All ancient religions were cosmologically oriented. They subordinated human, historic, and ethical interrelationships to processes of nature. Eric Voegelin summarizes this character of ancient cosmology and relates it to the uniqueness of biblical history. He states, "Without Israel there would be no history, but only the eternal recurrence of societies in cosmological form."[24] He continues, " 'eternal recurrence' is the symbol by means of which a cosmological civilization expresses (or rather can express if it be so minded) the experience of its own existence, the lasting and passing in the order of the cosmos. 'Eternal recurrence' is part of the cosmological form itself—it is not a category of historiography, nor will it ever have an historian."[25] Now it may be objected that Voegelin goes too far in saying that cosmological processes can never have a historian. However, once we grasp the point of the essential character of history as being defined and delineated by an ideal goal, then I believe the correctness of Voegelin's characterization of cyclical history—as not really history at all—can easily be seen. The Bible clearly and definitely separated man from nature. The Bible sees man as a spiritual, self-conscious being who has an inner life which gives him an ideal which is opposed to the actual and which he must try to actualize through the process of history.

Cosmological speculation is characteristic even of Greek modes of thinking. The Greeks viewed man as the microcosm of the macrocosm,[26] and the macrocosm, the cosmos, was one of eternal recurrence and continual cyclical processes.[27] It was the cyclical natural process which dominated Greek cosmic and historical speculation. It was an attempt to include man in history under the category of natural events. The idea of eternal recurrence dominated Greek thought down through the breakdown of the post-Aristotelian Stoic and Epicurean philosophies. Windelband points this out when he states that "every form of world construction must ultimately repeat itself . . . in this doctrine Epicurus agrees with the Stoics who taught a plurality of worlds in co-existence by following one another in time . . . completely alike even to the last detail of particular formation and particular events."[28]

One of the basic problems of Greek philosophy was the relation of man to the cyclical process of nature. The only hope for man is the soul's contemplation of the imperishable ideal. Historically, however, man cannot escape the wheel of eternal recurrence.[29] This is especially poignant in Plato's *Republic*, where the ideal state is described by Plato as "the city whose home is the ideal, for I think that it can be found nowhere on earth. Well, said I [Socrates], perhaps there is a pattern laid up in heaven for him who wishes to contemplate it and so beholding it constitute himself its citizen. But it makes no difference whether it exists now or ever will come into being."[30]

But even this ideal state, if it ever comes into being, cannot endure. It, too, must be engulfed in the cyclical process. As Socrates says, "Hard in truth it is for a state thus constituted to be shaken and disturbed, but since for everything that has come into being, destruction is appointed, not even such a fabric as this will abide for all time but it shall surely be dissolved."[31]

Once we have distinguished between cosmology and history, a second aspect of the significance of the Messianic Age can be discerned. In the Bible the cosmological and the historical are not only clearly separated, but in some important respects they are antagonistic. As long as the gods were aspects of nature, then this separation could not have been conceived. But with the idea of God as a transcendent being, the moral character of man was no more confused with natural processes since, as Cassirer states, "in the basic prophetic view there can be no relation between man and God other than the spiritual-ethical relation between the I and the Thou; everything that does not belong to this fundamental relation now loses its religious value. In the moment when the religious function, having discovered the world of pure inwardness, withdraws from the world of outward, natural existence, this existence loses its soul, as it were, and is degraded to the level of a dead 'thing.' Thus, the images taken from this sphere cease to be an expression of the spiritual and divine and turn into its antithesis pure and simple. The sensuous image and the whole sensuous phenomenal world must be divested of their symbolic meaning, for this alone can no longer be expressed in any material image."[32] What man ought to do is actualize the Messianic Age. This means the transformation of the natural. It means reshaping the natural in terms of the moral. History implies the conquering of the natural world, a reshaping of man and nature in terms of the ideal of justice and peace. The Messianic Age is the ideal goal which ought to be realized, and the desacralized natural or cosmological realm becomes the datum or the matrix of this transformation.

The historical and the cosmological have been shown to be independent and opposed to one another. We can now restate our original characterization of biblical thought in terms of ideal-actual in a sharper manner.

The ideal as characterized by the Messianic Age cannot be conceived as part of natural law, and in the same way the natural is only potentially moral. What is, is amoral and functions according to its own laws, irrespective of man and his well-being; what ought to be is moral and views man as the center and pivot of all that is. Man in fact is *not* the center of the universe, yet morally he *ought* to be its center. This antagonism between the normative, which is postulated by the historical, and the descriptive, which is characterized by the cosmological, is seen in a most explicit contrast in the Book of Job.

The Book of Job

The Book of Job is characteristic of the tragic and heroic dimensions implicit in the realization of the Messianic Age.[33]

The most direct manner of dealing with the problem and teaching of the Book of Job is to determine why the epilogue announces that the Friends have not spoken correctly of God as Job (His servant) has (42:7–9) and, therefore, must offer up a burnt offering for their sin. What constitutes the Friends' sin? It would *seem* that the Friends have defended God and have stood up for Him against Job's challenge. Their thesis can be summarized as follows:

First, God is just, and thus no innocent person ever perished and no wicked person ever triumphed. Second, Job must have sinned. Otherwise, God would not be punishing him. The only alternative is that God is unjust, and this would be blasphemy. Although at first it may seem otherwise, if one persists, he will discover that God's justice does indeed operate in this world as it does in all His doings in the natural and human realm.

Third, the Friends affirm that man is finite and of necessity imperfect, and therefore is in no condition to challenge God or to question God's ways.

Job maintains, first of all, that he is innocent, and even if God were to slay him, he would still definitely proclaim his integrity. He states, "I will defend my ways to His face." Second, he challenges their basic proposition and maintains that often the wicked do prosper and the righteous do suffer, and that God does not seem to hearken to the prayers of the oppressed. Third, he states that the Friends are whitewashers and liars and speak falsely for God, but that God will vindicate him.

Two completely alien positions are expressed here. Implicit in the arguments of the Friends and the refrain that runs through all of their speeches is that justice is a fact and to deny it is to blaspheme God. They affirm that God's goodness completely depends on the actuality of rewards and punishments in this world. Job accuses them of lying (13:4) and speaking deceitfully for God. He defends his integrity in the face of all, and finally turns to God to vindicate him and to resolve his perplexity. Why do the good suffer? (And here we are aware that in Job's case it is the best man, the most righteous, suffering the worst fate.) (1:8, 11–12; 2:3–6) How reconcile the reality of the ideal of justice with the fact of injustice? What are the roles of God and man in all this? Job has confronted God, as in a lawsuit, asking him to "call and I will answer, or let me speak and do Thou reply to me" (13:22). God, however, is silent (19:7), and so Job asks in a crescendo of questions ·(31:5 ff.), "If I have walked with falsehood, if my step had turned aside from the way and my heart had gone after my eyes, if my heart had been enticed by a woman." After vindicating his conduct with respect to personal morality, Job turns to his relation to his fellowman. "If I have rejected the cause of my man servant"; "If I have withheld anything that the poor desired or have eaten my morsel alone"; "If I have seen anyone perish for lack of clothing." Now he turns to his own values and ideals: "If I made gold my trust . . . If I have rejoiced because my wealth was great"; "If I had rejoiced at the ruin of him that hated me."

The crescendo of questions addressed by Job to God plainly

demonstrates his integrity and innocence. *If* he had done any of these, then his punishment would be just, but he is innocent and God is to declare to him wherein he has done wrong.

The Friends are left far behind. They can say nothing. Now it is God's turn. As in a lawsuit, God must either answer or Himself pose questions for Job to answer. And finally, God's voice issues forth from the whirlwind: "Where were you when I laid the foundations of the earth?" "Who determined its measurements?" "Have you walked in the recesses of the deep?" "Have the gates of death been revealed to you?" "Who has cleft a channel for the torrents of rain . . . to bring rain in a land where no man is, on the desert where there is no man, to satisfy the waste and desolate land?" God begins by asking questions concerning the laws operating in nature. He then turns to the order of the animal world: "Can you hunt the prey for the lion or satisfy the appetite of the young lion?" "Who provides for the raven its prey?" "Who has let the wild ass go free?" Nature and animal life are so diversified and vast that the mere listing of these questions undercuts man's belief that the whole universe and everything in it functions for the sake of man and is created expressly for his needs. On the contrary, nature and animal life have their own laws, which are separate and unrelated to man's needs. But even more, nature is indifferent to the morality so central to man. "The wings of the ostrich wave proudly, but are they the pinions and plumage of love? She leaves her eggs on the ground, forgetting that a foot may crush them. . . . She deals cruelly with her young." "And the eagle, he spies out his prey and the young ones suck up blood." The brunt of these questions is to show overwhelmingly both the variety and diversity of existence and also its amoral character. Nature and animal life do not function morally. The culmination comes when God confronts Job directly: "Will you condemn me that *you* may be justified. . . . Deck yourself with majesty and dignity, clothe yourself with glory and splendor, look on everyone that is proud and abase him, look on everyone that is proud and bring him low, and tread down the wicked where they stand. Hide them all in the dust together, bind their faces in the world below, then will I also acknowledge to you *that your own right hand can give you victory.''*

Job responds. He says he now understands and that he repents. What does Job now understand? What is God's answer? First, that man is not the center of the world. Second, that the order of the world is amoral. Third, that God has placed upon *man* the task of "treading the wicked." *Man* must do the work on earth. *He* must realize that it is his "own hand that will give him victory." It is not up to God to do man's work. Fourth, that the world is unfinished, and that man must strive to *become* for he is not *yet* its center. It is only in an unfinished universe, one that is in the making, one that is not yet won for God and man, that man can indeed have a task and a function. Yet the good suffer and the best suffer most because it is the just and true and righteous that take upon themselves the task of bringing justice and truth in the world. When man has achieved his task, only then will a new heaven and a new earth appear together with a new heart and a new covenant, then the whole earth will be full of the knowledge of God and the lion will eat straw like the ox, then none shall be afraid, then God shall be one and His name shall be one.

If we return to our original question, what constitutes the sin of the Friends, the answer is now clear. The sin of the Friends is threefold. First, they affirm that man indeed *is* at the center of the universe, and thus assume that the natural and the moral are one. In fact, as we have seen, Job's protest and the answer of God demonstrate that they are not in fact one but must be made one. Second, they deny the very nature of man's task. For them man has no self-transcending, nature-transforming historical task. They thus deny what is at the heart of the prophetic concept of man—that *he* is the instrument for the realization of the Messianic goal, a historical and not purely cosmological being. Third, they make trivial the suffering and agony, the tragic pathos, endured by the just man who is the agent for the realization of the good. The Friends want *God* to do *man's* work, and thus they have not spoken correctly as Job, who recognizes injustice yet sticks to his task and to his ideal despite the utmost agony and the most intense suffering. Job is the *'eved Adonai*, the servant of God par excellence, and he symbolizes to us the historic transformations that nature and man must accomplish if God' world is to emerge, to be brought into being.

Job is called the servant of the Lord and is symbolic of the suffering Israel who has a mission which can only involve suffering. The concept of the servant of God comes to completion in the heroic and terrifying servant passages in Second Isaiah. There God states, "Hearken to me you who know righteousness, the people in whose heart is My law. Fear not the reproach of men." Israel, the servant of God, is to be a light unto the nations that God's salvation may reach to the ends of the earth (Isa. 49:6). In these servant passages the promise that was made to Abraham is transmuted into the broadest and most universal context. Now a law will go forth from God and His justice for a light unto the people. The servant of God is to carry God's law, he is to declare God's kingdom. His mouth is like a sharp sword (49:2). He has the tongue of them that are taught (50:4). God's servant, Israel, must affirm God in the world, must bear witness undismayed to the ideal goal of brotherhood and peace. As Professor Slonimsky so strikingly says, "The assertion of God in a godless world is the supreme act of religion. It is a continuing of the act of creation on the highest plane. It adds slowly to the area and substance of the Kingdom of God and to the stature of God, the translation of God as ideal and vision into the God of empirical embodiment and of power. Man in whom God's creative effort had achieved a provisional pinnacle, so to speak, God's own self-consciousness of His aims, becomes from now on God's confronting partner, and the two together a re-enforcing polarity of give and take. They become allies in the most redoubtable of all struggles, and for the greatest of all stakes. They are inevitably lovers, and both of them tragic heroes. But, in a very real sense the fate of God and of the future rests on the heroism of man."

The suffering servant in Second Isaiah is patterned after Job and Jeremiah, but is symbolic and stands for all good men and true, the saints and chosen of God who redeem the world.

NOTES

I would like to express my thanks to Rabbi Robert Seltzer for many illuminating suggestions and useful comments which helped me in the preparation of this paper. An earlier version of this paper was delivered as the first Mortimer M. Taube Memorial Lecture, Washington, D. C.

1. Erich Auerbach, *Mimesis,* p. 14.

2. This is not mentioned by Auerbach; however, it fits in well with his overall position. This comparison, which Auerbach so well illustrates, was first suggested to me by Dr. Atlas.

3. Auerbach, *Mimesis,* p. 19.

4. Ibid., p. 10.

5. Ibid., p. 14.

6. Gen. 47:9.

7. Isa. 6.

8. Isa. 22; cf. S. Blank, in *Hebrew Union College Annual,* 1956, pp. 84 ff.

9. E. Cassirer, *Philosophy of Symbolic Forms,* 2:120. The statement of Hermann Cohen is here quoted. Cassirer's whole discussion on pp. 119–20 and 240–41 is extremely important and gives further evidence of the basic thesis of this paper.

10. Baeck, *The Pharisees and Other Essays,* p. 140.

11. Isa. 6; cf. Buber, *Prophetic Faith.*

12. Jer. 26; Blank, *Jeremiah.*

13. See my "Dimensions of Jewish Ethics," *American Judaism.*

14. See Y. Kaufmann, *The Religion of Israel,* ed. and trans. M. Greenberg, pp. 343–451.

15. The date 701 B.C.E. is generally given by biblical scholars.

16. Mic. 6.

17. Amos 5; cf. Isa. 1, Jer. 7.

18. Isa. 40.

19. 1 Kings 19.

20. W. Eichrodt, *Man in the Old Testament,* p. 30.

21. F. M. Cornford, *From Religion to Philosophy,* p. 115, "Nature dispeopled of Gods is left free for science." Cf. Cassirer, *Philosophy of Symbolic Forms,* p. 421.

22. Mic. 4; cf. Isa. 2.

23. Isa. 11:6–9; cf. Hos. 2:18, Isa. 65:17–25; Zech. 14:6–9.

24. E. Voegelin, *Order and History,* 1:126.

25. Ibid., p. 127.

26. Eichrodt, *Man in the Old Testament,* p. 15; cf. E. Caird, *Evolution of Theology in Greek Philosophers,* chap. 17.
That man was viewed as the microcosm of the macrocosm can be seen to characterize the thought of Anaximander, Anaximenes (see Guthrie, *History of Greek Philosophy,* I:132), Democritus (see Guthrie, p. 208n.), Pythagorianism (Guthrie, p. 201), Heraclitus (Guthrie, p. 479), Empedocles (Guthrie, p. 209), and Plato (Guthrie, p. 210), cf. *Timeus* 47b.

The microcosm-macrocosm relation is closely connected to the cyclical character of natural process. We could cite Anaximander, Heraclitus (Guthrie, p. 458), and numerous others (see my essay, "Some Philosophical Aspects of Koheleth," *Dimension*, Fall 1966, and the sources cited there).

27. Cornford, *From Religion to Philosophy*, p. 8, cf. pp. 165–66, 176–77.
28. Windelband, *History of Philosophy*, p. 185.
29. See my essay, "Some Philosophical Aspects of Koheleth."
30. Plato, *Republic* 592b.
31. Ibid., 546a.
32. Cassirer, *Philosophy of Symbolic Forms*, p. 241.
33. For a strikingly similar, though independently arrived at, interpretation of the Book of Job, see Professor M. Tsevat's article, "The Meaning of the Book of Job," in *Hebrew Union College Annual*, 1966.

THE TWO LIVES OF HILLEL'S "SANDWICH"

WILLIAM G. BRAUDE

W E shall attempt to demonstrate that *Korek*, or "Hillel's sandwich" as it is popularly known, has two lives, one legal, the other liturgical.

The legal life of Hillel's "sandwich," as set forth in a host of Tannaitic and Amoraic dicta, is complex and made up of elements which contradict one another. Thus, to begin with, it is not clear what ingredients went into the "sandwich." According to one version, Hillel used to take an olive-size of Passover lamb, matza, and bitter herbs and eat the three together in keeping with the command that the Passover be eaten *with unleavened bread and bitter herbs* (Num. 9:11). [1] According to another version, likewise based on Numbers 9:11, Hillel ate matza and bitter herbs together but not the olive-size of Passover lamb. [2] Hillel's colleagues, the Sages, differed, believing as they did that Passover's three elements—lamb, matza, and bitter herbs— must be eaten separately, each act of eating being deemed as fulfilling a distinct command; and, said they, when two or three commands are performed together, one nullifies the others. [3]

Concerning the practice of Hillel with regard to his "sandwich," further differences appear in post-Talmudic analysis: According to some, Hillel believes the "sandwich" to be indispensable; according to others, the "sandwich" is required only in the first instance, but if matza and bitter herbs are eaten separately, the Passover precept concerning lamb, matza, and herbs is deemed by Hillel to have been performed properly. Post-Talmudic analysis differs also with regard to the Sages' opinion: According to some authorities, the Sages opine that Hillel's "sandwich" contravenes the prescription that matza and bitter herbs, separately ordained, be eaten separately; according to other authorities, either way the matza and herbs—together or separately—are acceptable; according to still others, the Sages concede the need for the "sandwich," but should matza and bitter herbs be eaten separately, the precept is nevertheless deemed to have been acceptably performed.[4]

Since the law was not decided either in keeping with the Sages or in keeping with Hillel, the norm is to follow both practices, one after the other.[5] Accordingly, nowadays, just before serving the meal, "The benediction ending 'Who bringest forth bread from the earth' is followed by the benediction ending 'concerning the eating of unleavened bread.' Whereupon the unleavened bread is dipped into *hăroset* and eaten. The benediction ending 'Concerning the eating of bitter herbs' follows next, and bitter herbs are dipped into *hăroset* and eaten. The eating of bitter herbs is a commandment based on the authority of the Scribes.[6] Then [in keeping with Hillel's practice] unleavened bread and bitter herbs are folded together, are dipped into *hăroset* and eaten [reclining as at a banquet][7] without reciting any benediction, as a reminder of the Temple."[8]

So much for the legal aspects of Hillel's "sandwich." We now come to the liturgical pattern in the Passover Haggadah, where the eating of the sandwich is introduced by the formula: "REMINDER OF THE TEMPLE: after Hillel. While the Temple yet stood, Hillel introduced a custom of his own into the Seder service: he would put together a piece of matza and a piece of bitter herb, and eat them together in literal fulfillment of the verse in the Torah: 'They shall be deemed as eating the Passover lamb even though they consume only matzas and bitter herbs' (Num. 9:11)."[9]

To understand the formula's full significance it is necessary to examine its every detail. The phrase "Reminder of the Temple" is employed in connection with a number of practices and observances similarly motivated. Thus the phrase is employed with regard to the special reading in Scripture on the Sabbath preceding the New Moon of Adar, at which time, during the days of the Temple, there began the announcement that the half-shekel for the purchase of daily offerings was due. On that Sabbath the supplementary lesson in the Pentateuch was Exodus 30:11–16 with its injunction to levy the half-shekel head tax for the Tabernacle, and ultimately for the Temple.[10] But even after the Temple's destruction, the practice of reading Exodus 30:11–16 on the Sabbath preceding the New Moon of Adar—the Sabbath known as Šĕḳalim—continued for the sake of Remembrance of the Temple.[11] So, too, the present practice of counting the Omer now that the Omer, the sheaf of wave-offering, is no longer possible, continues, so it is said for the sake of Remembrance of the Temple.[12] This phrase is also employed with regard to the lulab cluster which used to be carried seven days in the Temple and only one day in the provinces. However, "After the Temple was destroyed, Rabban Johanan ben Zakkai ordained that in the provinces the lulab cluster should be carried seven days in Remembrance of the Temple."[13] Then, too, with the lulab cluster in hand "the altar used to be encircled on Sukkot's seventh day seven times."[14] And, accordingly, Maimonides asserts: "It has long been the custom in Israel everywhere to place in the middle of the synagogue the Ark of the Law and to circle it each day in the same manner as the altar used to be circled, in Remembrance of the Temple."[15] Then, too, nowadays on the seventh day of Sukkot "one or more withes of willow are taken up and struck against the ground or against an article of furniture two or three times in Remembrance of the usage in the Temple."[16] Finally, when Hanukkah candles are lit in the synagogue it is enjoined in Remembrance of the Temple that the lamp containing them be placed at the synagogue's south wall, the side where the Temple lampstand used to be.[17]

The aforementioned practices and observances initiated in Remembrance of the Temple are said to be rooted in Scripture, where "God is quoted as saying *I will restore health unto thee, and I will heal thee of thy wounds . . . because* [*the nations*] *have called thee an outcast: 'She is withered, there is no need for anyone even to remember her'* (Jer. 30:17). Accordingly it is you, O children of Israel, [who like your God in heaven] are to bring Zion's Temple to remembrance."[18]

During none of the aforementioned practices, each intended to bring Zion's Temple to remembrance, were the words "In Remembrance of the Temple" actually uttered—they were and are implied, but not uttered. Thus the worshipers who carried the lulab cluster during the seven days of Sukkot were not enjoined to say right out "Reminder of the Temple: after Rabban Johanan ben Zakkai." But—and this is the one exception—they who ate Hillel's "sandwich" were required before eating it to say "Reminder of the Temple: after Hillel." What does this one exception signify? That all the other practices—the reading of Exodus 30:11–16 on the Sabbath preceding the New Moon of Adar, the counting of the Omer, the carrying of the lulab cluster for the seven days of Sukkot, the circling of the Ark of the Law, the striking of withes of willow against the ground on Sukkot's seventh day, and finally the placing of the Hanukkah lamp at the synagogue's south wall—all these practices were essentially no more than remembrances partaking only vaguely of the character of the original observance. Not so Hillel's "sandwich." In its liturgical use it was intended to celebrate, in modified form to be sure, but nevertheless to celebrate, the Passover as it had been celebrated in the days of the Temple with the matza, symbol of freedom, all but taking the place of Passover's lamb,[19] and the bitter herbs, symbol of sorrows experienced and overcome in the Egyptian past and now experienced and ultimately to be overcome in the Roman present.

A legal discussion in a Tannaitic Midrash appears to sustain our liturgical interpretation of Hillel's "sandwich." The discussion goes thus: "*They shall eat the flesh* [*of the lamb*] *in that night, roast with fire; and unleavened bread; with bitter herbs they shall eat it* (Exod. 12:8). Whence the proof that when there are no matzas and no bitter herbs Jews can discharge their obligation solely by the eating of the Passover lamb? From the aforecited verse's conclusion, *they shall [under any circumstances] eat it.* And whence on the other hand the proof that where there is no Passover lamb Jews can discharge their obligation by the eating of matzas and bitter herbs? From reasoning as follows: Eating the Passover lamb is a mandatory duty, and eating matzas and bitter herbs is also a mandatory duty. Now, inasmuch as it has been proved that when there are no matzas and bitter herbs Jews can discharge their obligation solely by eating the Passover lamb, it is logical to suppose that when Jews have no Passover lamb they can likewise discharge their obligation by eating matzas and bitter herbs."[20]

We may assume that the Tannaitic discussion just cited reflects the intent of the liturgical formula ascribed to Hillel. In that formula matza is not taken as "the bread of affliction" but is meant to evoke the memory of the unleavened cakes of dough, which on account of the Jews' precipitous departure from Egypt could not be leavened; and so, like the Passover lamb, the matza in the Hillel "sandwich" signifies freedom from bondage in Egypt, and prayerfully, from the present bondage. By way of expressing assurance that such freedom from Rome was bound to come, certain legists assert that the matza eaten in Hillel's "sandwich" be not dipped in *ḥăroset,* the condiment associated with the mortar and bricks of bondage; and that the bitter herbs in Hillel's "sandwich" be eaten reclining as at a banquet.[21]

Ancillary proof that the liturgical intent of Hillel's "sandwich" was to provide a surrogate for the Passover lamb and its proclamation of the birth of the Jewish people comes from the verse Numbers 9:11, which is cited as the text supporting Hillel's practice.

To appreciate the significance of the way this particular verse is used, we will quote again the formula in the Passover Haggadah which precedes the eating of the "sandwich": "REMINDER OF THE TEMPLE: after Hillel. While the Temple yet stood, Hillel introduced a custom of his own into the Seder service: he would put together a piece of matza and a piece of bitter herb, and eat them together in literal fulfillment of the verse in the Torah: 'They shall be deemed as eating the Passover lamb even though they consume only matzas and bitter herbs' (Num. 9:11).''[22] The particular verse cited in the formula occurs in a passage which provides a second or a secondary Passover on the fourteenth day of Iyar for those who for one reason or another were unable to participate in the celebration at the appointed time on the fourteenth day of Nisan. The provision for such celebration is set forth in the words *If any man of you or of your generations shall be unclean by reason of a dead body, or be on a journey afar off . . . he shall keep the Passover unto the Lord in the second month on the fourteenth day at dusk* (Num. 9:10). Now for those uttering Hillel's liturgical formula, their observance of Passover, handicapped as it was by the loss of the Temple, fitted Numbers 9, where a second or secondary Passover was introduced. The generation or generations after the Temple's destruction may well have applied the words *unclean by reason of a dead body, or be on a journey afar off* to themselves. By reason of their sins they too, they felt, were deprived of the Temple with its Passover lamb, supreme symbol and expression of Israel's freedom. In the parallel verse, in Exodus 12:8, commentators sensed an intimation that certainly the eating of bitter herbs[23] and possibly even the eating of matzas was dependent upon the use of the Passover lamb. And so there was fear that such an intimation all but suggested the abandonment of the rites of Passover. The ultimate opinion, to be sure, is that the eating of matzas on the first night of Passover was an obligation enjoined in Scripture. Here is how the problem was stated: ''We know that such indeed was the character of the obligation when the Temple existed. Whence do we know that the same kind of obligation continues now that the Temple is not in existence? From the verse *At even ye shall eat unleavened bread* (Exod. 12:18). Thus Writ made the eating of matza a permanent obligation.''[24]

Wrestlings such as these point to Tannaitic and Amoraic efforts against those who in despair after the Temple's destruction all but suggested, as has already been stated, the abolition of Passover's rites.

Certain Tannaim were even more daring in their efforts

against such despair. Thus Thaddeus of Rome introduced among the Jews of Rome the Passover eve custom of eating "helmeted" goats[25]—not lambs, but goats—roasted whole in the manner in which the Passover lamb was roasted, with the entrails and the legs on the head like a helmet. Thaddeus suggested roasting goats possibly because goats were used less frequently as offerings and certainly were less prominently associated with the Passover. By his use of goats, Thaddeus presumably meant to allay any suspicion that he intended to bring offerings outside the Temple. Even though the Sages protested Thaddeus' innovation, nevertheless, in Rome the Jewish community apparently followed Thaddeus, as evident from Josephus' saying "To this day we"—and he was writing his book in Rome—"keep the [Passover] sacrifice in the same manner."[26] Not, to be sure, precisely in the same manner. But to ordinary people the roasting of the "helmeted" goat appeared to simulate the Passover offering.[27]

One should note that Rabban Gamaliel II (80–120 C.E.) likewise permitted roasting "helmeted" goats on Passover eve.[28] "It would seem," so Gedaliah Alon points out, "that Rabban Gamaliel sought as much as possible to maintain the Passover offering even after the Temple's destruction. Not, to be sure, an actual or valid offering since after the destruction slaughtering the lamb before the altar and dashing its blood or burning parts of it on the altar were no longer possible."[29] In keeping with his view, however, Rabban Gamaliel once said to his slave Tabi, "Go and roast the Passover offering for us on the grill."[30]

In the Land of Israel as well as in Rome, the practice of bringing "surrogate" Passover offerings ceased. Nevertheless, some Jews apparently continued to eat roast meat as symbolic of the Passover offering. Thus, according to a Mishnah, the third question a son would ask his father on Passover eve was: "Why on other nights do we eat flesh roasted, stewed, or cooked, but on this night all roast?"[31]

It may well be that after the destruction of the Temple the pressures pro and contra roasting flesh, or eating matza and bitter herbs on Passover, were so many and so varied that they resulted—as said at the beginning of this essay—in legal teachings that were mutually contradictory. In its liturgical formulation, Hillel's "sandwich" apparently intended to omit the use of roast flesh on Passover and to regard the matza as its surrogate.

Hillel, who flourished in the early part of the first century C.E., was not alone in foreseeing the destruction of the Temple. Forty years before the event, R. Zadok, it is said, began observing fasts to ward off by prayer Jerusalem's destruction,[32] the coming of which was presaged by a congeries of somber signs. Thus during those forty years "the lot 'For the Lord'[33] did not come up in the High Priest's right hand; nor did the crimson-colored strap become white; nor did the westernmost light continue to shine; and the doors of the hall containing the golden altar would [as though welcoming the enemy] eerily open by themselves."[34] Like R. Zadok, Hillel read these signs as predicting the destruction of the Temple. Apparently he felt that rites such as "helmeting" goats or roasting flesh on Passover to evoke memories of the Temple, whose destruction was certain, would not do. But in a bold and imaginative way he proposed that the matza and the bitter herbs be eaten together to symbolize or represent the Paschal offering, the matza serving as surrogate for the lamb.

In fine: Hillel's "sandwich," the custom which, according to liturgical tradition, he introduced on his own while the Temple was still standing, was a declaration that as in Egypt so again under Rome—the bitterness of bondage will cease and Jews will be free again. His "sandwich" thus anticipated the comprehensive measures which, in the years following the destruction of the Temple, Hillel's disciple Rabban Johanan ben Zakkai was to ordain—the disciple whom Hillel in his prescience characterized as "father of wisdom" and "father of generations to come."[35]

NOTES

1. See Tos Pes 2[1]:22, ed. Lieberman (New York 5722/1962), *Móed*, p. 150; Mĕkilta de-R. Simeon ben Yoḥai, ed. Melamed (Jerusalem, 5715/1945), p. 13; P.Hal 1:1,57b; Rashi and Rashbam on B.Pes 115a; and Rashi on B.Zeb 79a.

2. See B.Pes 115a; B. Zeb 79a; and Maimonides, Code III, v, viii, 6–8 (Yale Judaica Series, *14*, 356–57).

3. In the days of the Temple—so it is averred in the Palestinian Talmud— two biblically ordained commands performed simultaneously would be deemed to nullify each other. After the Temple's destruction, however, the bitter herb eaten without the Passover lamb is deemed a Rabbinic injunction, and as such does not nullify matza, which even after the Temple's destruction continues to be biblically ordained. The very opposite is taught in the Babylonian Talmud. There it is maintained that the rabbinically enjoined bitter herb, when eaten together with matza, nullifies the latter, which continues to be biblically ordained. See Saul Lieberman, *Tosefta kipĕšuṭah* (New York, 5722/1962), *Móed*, 4, 510.

4. See *Enṣiklopedya Talmudit* (Tel Aviv, 5715/1955), 1, 363, s.v. *Akilat maror*.

5. B.Pes 115a.

6. So also in his *Sefer ha-Miswot*, Positive Commandments 56 (Charles B. Chavel, Maimonides, *The Commandments* [Soncino Press, London and New York], 1,. 67). Maimonides comes to such a conclusion in the face of considerable Tannaitic opinion to the contrary, e.g., Tos Pes 2[1]: 22, ed. Lieberman, *Móed*, p. 150; Mekilta dĕ-R. Ishmael, ed. Horovitz-Rabin (Frankfurt, 1931), *Bo*, 6, p. 20, and n. 2. The Tannaitic opinion, which even after the Temple's destruction regards the eating of bitter herbs as based on the authority of Scripture, is—as the writer hopes to demonstrate—important in the liturgical life of Hillel's "sandwich."

7. The prescription that during the eating of the "sandwich" there be *hesebah*, or reclining as at a banquet, is stated in Šulhan'aruk Orah hayyim 475. Others—Maimonides, R. Zedekiah's Šibbole hal-leket, 218, and R. Eliezer of Worms' Rokeah, 283—do not prescribe reclining.

8. Maimonides, Code III, V, viii, 8 (Yale Judaica Series, 14, 357).

9. JV; *they shall eat it with unleavened bread*. For the translation of the formula introducing Hillel's *Korek*, cf. *Haggadah of Passover* trans. Maurice Samuel (New York, 1942), p. 32. See also Daniel Goldschmidt, *Haggadah šel Pesah* (Jerusalem, 1947), ad loc.

10. See Még 3:4, and Pesikta Rabbati 10:1 (Yale Judaica Series, *18*, 1, 168–69).

11. Aaron hal-lewi of Barcelona, Sefer ha-ḥinnuk, 105.

12. See B.Men 66a and Rashi, s.v. "Amemar."

13. Suk 3:12; RH 4:3.

14. Suk 4:5.

15. See Midrash on Psalms 26:5 (Yale Judaica Series, *13, 1,* 359); Maimonides, Code III, VI, vii, 23 (Yale Judaica Series, *14*, 402); and Ṭur Orah hayyim 660.

16. Suk 4:6, and Maimonides, Code III, VI, vii, 22 (Yale Judaica Series, *14*, 402).

17. See Ṭur Oraḥ ḥayyim 671.

18. In JV Jer. 30:17 reads *Because they have called thee an outcast: "She is Zion, there is none that careth for her!"* But Zion can mean "the land of, or the Temple of Zion," or "that which is dry and withered." The comment is found in B.Suk 41a and RH 30a.

19. On the lamb as a symbol of freedom and daring, see Pesikta Rabbati 15:23 (Yale Judaica Series, *18, 1,* 337–38); and Pesikta de-Raḇ Kahana, ed. Mandelbaum 5:17.

20. See Měḳilta dě-R. Ishmael, *Boʼ,* 6, ed. Horovitz-Rabin (Frankfurt am Main, 1931), p. 20 and note; and Yalḳuṭ Exod. 197 (ed. Saloniki, 1521–27). Cf. Meḳilta de-R. Ishmael, ed. Lauterbach (Philadelphia, 1933), *1,* 47–48.

21. See Isserles' second gloss in Šulḥan ʻaruḵ Oraḥ ḥayyim 475; and Ṭur Oraḥ ḥayyim 475, where Abraham ben Nathan of Lunel's Manhig is quoted as saying that one should recline while eating the Hillel "sandwich," which is the practice prescribed, in the Šulḥan ʻaruḵ Oraḥ ḥayyim ad loc., as normative.

22. Menahem Mendel Kasher endeavors to prove that in the Passover Haggadah and in other Rabbinic texts the citation of Num. 9:11 is a *lapsus calami*. According to him the proof text should be Exod. 12:8, which reads *They shall eat the flesh [of the lamb] in that night roast with fire, and unleavened bread; with bitter herbs they stall eat it.* See his Torah šělemah, Exodus 10–11 (New York, 1946), pp. 97–99, and 210–13. But since the substitution he proposes involves emending a great many texts, it is difficult to accept.

23. See Naḥmanides on Exod. 12:8.

24. See B.Pes 120a.

25. See B.Pes 53a and Soncino translation, p. 260, n. 2; and Beṣah 23a.

26. See Josephus, *Antiquities 2, 14,* 6 (313); and Jean Juster, *Les Juifs dans L'Empire Romain* (Paris, 1914), *1,* 357, n. 1.

27. See Saul Lieberman, *Tosefta kipěšuṭah* (New York, 5722/1962), *Moʼeḏ, 5,* 959, n. 38.

28. See Beṣah 2:7.

29. Gedaliah Alon, *Tolědoṭ Ha-Yěhudim be-Ereṣ Yiśraʼel bi-těḵufaṭ ha-Misnah we-ha-Talmud* (Tel Aviv, 5713/1952), *1,* 165.

30. Pes 7:2.

31. Pes 10:4. Since the third question is phrased the same way in Genizah fragments, Alon (ibid.) maintains that the Mishnah reflects not a time prior to the Temple's destruction but one following it.

32. B.Giṭ 56a. Jesus also is said to have foreseen the Temple's destruction. See Matt. 23:38 and Luke 13:34.

33. In the urn containing the two lots for the two goats made use of in the rites of the Day of Atonement. One lot was inscribed "For the Lord," the other, "For Azazel." See Yoma 4:1.

34. See B.Yoma 39b.

35. See P.Neḏ 5:7, 39b.

THE HEALTH GUILDS, THE PUBLIC INTEREST, AND THE MALPRACTICE DILEMMA

CARLETON B. CHAPMAN

THE health professions have, for some years, been living amidst a whole series of crises. In the easy recollection of those not yet middle-aged, there have been the health-care crisis, the doctor-shortage crisis, and several varieties of crises having to do with the cost of health services; not to mention a large number of lesser health-oriented matters also—at times—called crises.

The medical malpractice crisis is the current case in point. It has already spawned a whole series of proposals and counter-proposals, most of them oversimplified, and some transparently slanted to the needs of various special-interest factions. None has as yet been based on anything like a careful analysis of the problem or an understanding of the system in the English-speaking world for the protection of the consumer of health services. The so-called solutions now being offered are all short-term—patchwork, in other words. But the total situation leads us inevitably to the most essential and the most neglected component of any long-term solution: a truly adequate and representative mechanism for bringing professional expertise to bear on public policy; for placing that expertise at the disposal of public officials when it is appropriate to do so; and, simultaneously, for protecting society from the effects of special-interest influences.

Our failure to evolve such a mechanism represents, in effect, a specific cultural arrest that has endured for six or seven hundred years. There are those like Milton Friedman, the economist, who say that by the mid-nineteenth century, the medieval guild system had been overthrown, but that, in recent decades, there has been a retrogression.[1] It might be more accurate to say that in some of our professional organizations, certain features of the medieval guild have never been overthrown at all. Restated, the problem is to establish a truly effective and equitable interface, in the public interest, between twentieth-century analogues of the craft guilds, on the one hand, and public authority, on the other. And the resolution of this problem is where the main action in the health professions is likely to be in the last quarter of the twentieth century.

The System for Protecting the Consumer against Substandard Professional Services

It is a problem that extends far beyond the confines of medical malpractice and, for that matter. of the health professions in their entirety. But the medical malpractice problem provides an appropriate and logical entrée into the larger arena. And the first step is to note that the social system underlying malpractice law and litigation is a dual proposition.

It possesses a legal, or common law, component, which is usually represented as the system itself. But this is to overlook the other, quite indispensable, component: the professional guild, which by its nature has from the beginning introduced an inevitable element of conflict of interest. The fundamental fact is simple enough: public authority has always, for many purposes, had to depend on the expertise of the professional guild; and while conflict of interest has from time to time been offset, it has never been eliminated altogether. And that fact, in turn, inevitably flows from the most basic and fundamental characteristic of the craft guild: its primary obligation and its only real accountability are to its membership and not to the public at large. Where the public interest and the interest of the professional guild run parallel, the guild's contribution to the public good may be magnificent. But when the guild's interests and the public's interest diverge, the guild must inevitably look after its own. Indeed, if it does not do so, it sooner or later fails as an organization. It's as simple as that; it was true in the Middle Ages, is true now, and will still be true as we enter the twenty-first century.

The basic common law of malpractice was largely complete, at least in broad principle, by the end of the fourteenth century.* There were already precedents that required the physician to be diligent, to avoid negligence, and, in effect, to do all he could for his patient. But he was not required to effect cure or to possess extraordinary knowledge and skill. He was liable, however, if his patient suffered injury as a result abandonment.[4-6]

But the judges of the King's High Courts were not able to define in meticulous detail the standards of knowledge and performance expected of a physician, horse doctor, or other provider. Medieval legal authorities, like their twentieth-century counterparts, were most reluctant to set such standards on their own; and not unreasonably some of them turned to the professional guilds for counsel. In 1354 London's highest civil authorities, sitting in judgment on a practitioner for alleged malpractice, called in three master surgeons as experts. These gentlemen said that if the practitioner had called in expert consultants (presumably themselves), the patient would most probably have been cured.[7, 8] The judgment was against the unfortunate practitioner, and fifteen years later, the symbiotic

---

*The most pertinent statement was made by John Cavendish, Chief Justice of the Court of the King's Bench, in 1374. It concerned the blacksmith's obligation to his horse-client but was actually part of a decision in the case of a human patient suing a surgeon. Cavendish had this to say: "If a blacksmith undertakes to heal my horse and if by his negligence, or by his neglecting to administer treatment at the proper time, the horse suffers permanent harm, it is right that he should be held guilty. But if he does all that he can, or treats him with all diligence, it is not right that he be held guilty even if the horse is not healed."[2, 3] It is only a short step from the Cavendish decision to later legal descriptions of the "average physician" acting responsibly and diligently.

relation between London's civil authorities and the Master Surgeons' Guild was made official by specific statute.[9]

It is not clear whether or not the authorities always accepted the verdicts of the guilds, but it is not difficult to imagine that practitioners who did not belong to the guilds, however competent they may have been, might fare badly when brought before such tribunals.

From the late Middle Ages in England to our own time a striking historical paradox has developed: the common law component of our professional malpractice system evolved, rapidly at first, then more slowly, into a highly effective social instrument for influencing standards of professional behavior; or, more accurately, for defining standards below which professional performance must not fall. But the other component, which for want of a better phrase may be called the guild-public interface, has evolved much, much more slowly—some would say that it has remained static—whether reference is to malpractice litigation, professional licensure and discipline, or health legislation. It has tended to be held synonymous with the guild itself, something which is, to an extent, a contradiction in terms.

Delegation of Authority to the Guild: The Record.

The legal record in Britain and in the United States bears striking witness to the occasional tendency of professional societies to use certain delegated authority in an arbitrary manner. In the early seventeenth century, for example, the Royal College of Physicians sought and obtained complete control over licensing physicians in London and was authorized to fine, and even to imprison, those who practiced without its sanction. To carry out this activity, the president and the board of censors were allowed by the statute to serve as a court of record; and there was soon trouble. It came to a head when one Dr. Bonham brought suit for damages, charging false imprisonment.[10] The case is famous in legal annals because it bore on basic constitutional issues having to do with the separation of powers.[11] But it also focused on the improper delegation of police and other powers by the state to a private body that was neither elected nor in any way publicly accountable. Chief Justice Edward Coke of the Court of Common Pleas said that the president and board of censors of the Royal College were not capable of functioning as a court of record, and that the College itself was in massive conflict of interest because it was allowed to retain half the fines it levied, the other half going to the king.[12]

In restrospect one wonders why the College accepted so uncritically such an onerous portion of the civil authorities' obligation to the public (which included trying and punishing physicians for malpractice). It is generally assumed that the College sought to have the authority delegated to it in order, guildlike, to protect its monopoly in London. No doubt that was one reason. But it would be unduly doctrinaire to assume that the parallel concern of the College for establishing and maintaining adequate standards of professional training and performance was wholly insincere and fraudulent. The really pertinent question is: What was the total cost to the College of attempting to function as a court of record? Althought I have no real evidence, I suspect that the long-term loss may have been far greater than the gain; that the task was infinitely more thankless than the officers and fellows of the College foresaw.

English common law came to America before the Revolution largely via Blackstone's writings,[13] and the English practice of delegating public authority to professional organizations was imported a bit later. It was in 1859 that the North Carolina State Medical Association was accorded, by legislative action, the power to appoint the state board of medical examiners. The board, in turn, elected its own officers, conducted licensing examinations, and revoked licenses for "immoral or unethical conduct," among other things. The board, for all practical purposes, was responsible not to the legislature but to the State Medical Association. In the last century various other patterns have emerged, ranging from the rather extreme North Carolina example to those which almost exclude professionals from licensing and disciplinary bodies.[14] But no one has yet discovered the optimal arrangement: the guild-public interface is still intermittently unstable and uneasy. Nor is the problem limited to the health professional organizations. More than half the states, Professor Walter Gellhorn tells us, have transformed the legal profession into an approximation of an autonomous guild.[15] And, speaking more generally, Grant says: "It is doubtful if many medieval guilds enjoyed a greater degree of independence. . . . [Modern statutes] have virtually erected these supposedly regulated callings into miniature governments."[16]

Time and time again, professional societies have been admonished by the courts for unfair or arbitrary use of delegated authority. A decision by Justice Marvin of the Supreme Court of the State of New York in 1857 made the law clear: "The power given, by statute, to medical societies, to make by-laws and regulations . . . is not an arbitrary, unlimited power. The by-laws, rules and regulations are not to be contrary to, nor inconsistent with, the laws of the state."[17] The principle has been affirmed many times since, but the guild orientation has very often been more influential than the admonitions of the courts. And when the medical fraternity, sometimes joined by insurance companies, conspired to make it difficult for patient-plaintiffs to obtain expert testimony in support of malpractice suits, [18–21] the courts understandably reacted. One state supreme court justice, for example, called attention to the "shocking unethical reluctance on the part of the medical profession in an action for malpractice. . . . A charge of malpractice is a serious . . . charge [against] a professional man, but it is not answered by an attempt to throttle justice."[22]

In most parts of the nation, the "conspiracy of silence" is largely a thing of the past. It has become less and less a factor as the locality rule* has been modified or abandoned in state after state.[23] But the traditional reluctance of a physician to testify against another physician is still very real.

---

*Which said that the level of knowledge and skill to which a physician had to conform was that of the locality in which he practiced. Testimony of physicians from other localities was usually not admissible.

The Guilds' Party Lines.

Since the malpractice dilemma, technically speaking, falls into the medicolegal category, one might assume that there must be some combination of medical and legal talent that is attacking the problem dispassionately and in detail. But so far, those spokesmen for the two professions who appear most often in print seem to be hewing rigidly to the guild line.

There are, for example, some segments of the doctor guild that would totally exempt all physicians from liability for negligence. One of the nation's most eminent medical authorities recently spoke of the contamination of medical care by the law of torts, and said that "in the best of worlds, the doctor-patient relationship should not be a subject for litigation . . . " The doctor guild, it is said, is best able to judge the validity of malpractice complaints and to discipline errant physicians.[24] Obviously this is hardly a balanced view. Such spokesmen, clearly, would like to preserve and even enhance the physician's relatively favorable economic status and, at the same time, protect him absolutely from having to pay damages to patients who are injured by negligent or otherwise substandard professional action.

As for the lawyer guild, the chief spokesmen to date seem to be past or present officers of various trial lawyers associations. To a man, they hold that there is no malpractice crisis, that the cause of malpractice is malpractice, and that the existing system should not in any way be altered. A scant three years ago, Richard M. Marcus, past-president of the Association of Trial Lawyers, said that doctors are paranoid about malpractice. The system, he implied, is optimal; and then he indulged in what must surely be the most wrong-headed prophecy of the century. He put it this way: "At present there are no localities where professional liability insurance is unavailable. Increasing numbers of insurers are going back into this field along with companies that never wrote this form of insurance before. As for premiums they did climb substantially in the latter half of the sixties but they've more or less levelled off now. . . . There seems little likelihood of large rate increases in the near future."[25]

This, mind you, was published exactly three years ago, at a time when the signs of the current crisis were clearly visible.

In the past few weeks another prominent trial lawyer characterized as "laughable" all suggestions that our present jury system for handling malpractice cases may be less than ideal. Her central theme, like that of most of her colleagues, was that there is nothing whatever wrong with our current system of malpractice law and litigation.[26]

The unanimity of the trial lawyers is, on the surface, surprising, lawyers being by nature and by profession a contentious lot. But the reason became quite clear when one takes note of the incomes some lawyers specializing in medical malpractice litigation are earning. One of them was quoted as saying that he had made upwards of a million dollars a year for ten years from such cases, one-third of each award being his usual compensation under the contingent fee arrangement. In what, at the time, was his most recent case, the total award to his client was $3,700,000, of which he, the lawyer, stood to receive over $1,230,000.[27] And about a year ago there was an even higher award—the highest on record—that came to $4,025,000, of which a quarter to a third goes to the lawyers.[28] There is, therefore, small wonder that the trial lawyers rise to such towering eloquence in their defence of the contingent fee system, which is illegal in Britain, Canada, Australia, New Zealand, and the great state of Maine; but not in the other forty-nine states.[29] The contingent fee system, and the use of juries for setting the size of awards in malpractice suits, serves the interests of many trial lawyers very well indeed. Obviously, we are not yet receiving a balanced or impartial estimate of the problem from our legal colleagues.

Malpractice: Cause and Cure

What can any reasonable person make of all this? The principal fact that emerges, it seems to me, is that guilds will be guilds, and that both rational analysis and long-term solution are not currently in prospect. The net effect of all the claims and counterclaims may well be that we will wind up with a comprehensive security law in which anyone suffering injury, whatever the cause, will be compensated by someone; and only rarely will anyone be held legally negligent. The consequences for the health professions of such a system should be a focal topic for another time and place. Suffice it to say that the special relationship between the health professional and the patient, something in which I am old-fashioned enough to retain some faith, would almost certainly be a casualty.

With the lawyers blaming the doctors and the doctors blaming the lawyers, the public—the consumer—is likely to blame both. But may it not be that *all three are to blame?* There are, after all, the past sins (e.g., the "conspiracy of silence") of the doctor guild; there are the present and past sins of the lawyer guild; and there is the cardinal sin of the consumer, who, more and more, hopes to convert appropriate compensation for something lost or suffered into opportunity for massive profit. The medical profession, being relatively favored in an economic sense, has become a target. And the trial lawyers, now so determined to maintain unchanged a system that serves them well, may confidently expect to be next in line.

As for the many patchwork propositions and reactions now being touted as cures for the malpractice dilemma, two brief comments may be in order. First, what about the use of the so-called doctors' strike as a means of forcing quick passage of acceptable legislation? Be it noted that, as yet, no one seems to be suggesting a full-fledged strike by doctors. As in Northern California, the proposal is mainly to defer all elective—but not emergency—surgery. Even so, strikes within the health professions constitute a very treacherous weapon; one that in this instance is not likely to produce the expected effect but may well produce some strange and unexpected ones. Many of those patients who can't have their elective surgery because of the strike, for example, may find that they get on remarkably well without the surgery. And those patients who actually suffer because of the strike will inevitably blame the striking doctor, not the lawyer or the legislator. Second, one hears increasingly about the need for a system by which health professionals are required to discipline their own errant members. But the guilds are not set up, as Dr. Bonham's case showed three centuries ago, to conduct airtight trials or to guarantee due process, even to their own members, especially where the basic right to make a living at one's chosen profession is concerned. Modification or withdrawal of that right belongs ultimately in the courts, and if the application of such disciplinary measures is currently unsatisfactory, the proper remedy is to bring pressure to bear on public authority to conduct itself more responsibly. In any case, the records of our major professional societies, both legal and medical, for disciplining their own members are most unconvincing. And although something is clearly wrong, the answer does not lie in making courts out of medical societies or out of other bodies that are not fully accountable and visible to the public.

Resolution and Conclusion

Finally, I return to the all-important matter of designing an effective mechanism for placing professional expertise of all sorts—including legal—fully and completely at the service of public authority, but without ignoring or succumbing to conflict of interest. This, after all, is the key to the long-term solution of the malpractice problem, among others.

The mere fact that such a mechanism has eluded us for so long should not, per se, be a deterrent to the rising generation of health professionals. Professor Gellhorn provides a key when he notes that the solution lies "in creating a responsible administrative body that . . . may employ vocationally experienced staff members and that should in all instances recruit suitable advisory groups from within the affected occupation."[30]

There are, in fact, a few models that can be studied, although none is precisely applicable. One such was the Office of Science and Technology, set up in its original form during World War II to provide the Executive Branch with expert counsel on scientific matters, including those involving health. The mechanism lifted qualified scientists out of the guild framework and more or less completely neutralized the effects of conflicts of interest. It was abolished two years ago, but if recent news accounts are accurate, it may soon be reestablished. On a lesser scale, there are the councils of the National Institutes of Health. They are designed to bring the guilds and the public together on equal terms and, depending on their specific membership, have often worked very well. There are no doubt others, but there are none that are broad enough to serve as templates for what is now needed.

Our professional organizations must for very good reasons remain guildlike in some respects. Yet it is overwhelmingly evident that they are now bound to participate in the design of new mechanisms for the service of the public need, and to agree under some circumstances to a considerable modification of their authority over some types of professional matters.

It may be said that present-day training for the health professions does not equip young people for activities of this sort. "No one speaks any more of the learned professions," says Carr-Saunders. "Training has taken the place of education. The modern professional man . . . is absorbed in restricted problems for which he seeks *ad hoc* solutions. . . . He is no longer able to . . . contribute usefully to the discussion of public affairs."[31] Perhaps this is so, although some of it is mere truism. But true or not, defects in education are both inevitable and generally remediable. My focus has been on what I've called a six-hundred-year cultural arrest, and I am of the view that it will have to be remedied before the century is out. I am also of the view that some of today's graduates will have a hand in devising the remedy and to that end will not hesitate to look as studiously and critically as need be at the law, the courts, public administration, and the historical background; which, collectively, is a special sort of continuing educational process that one carries out on his own and largely by his own efforts.

There are those who speak of the genius of the common law; and there are some who speak of the genius of the American democracy. In both cases this represents an extravagance of language that is self-serving, complacent, and even dangerous.

The common law and our democracy are marvelously pragmatic instruments that are also dynamic and flexible. But change and flexibility very often have to take place within some sort of framework of impartial and highly expert professional counsel. To provide it is the problem of the eighties and nineties.

NOTES

This paper was originally presented as the commencement address at Cornell University Medical College, Cornell University-New York Hospital School of Nursing, and Cornell University Graduate School of Medical Science, New York, May 28, 1975.

1. Milton Friedman, *Capitalism and Freedom* (Chicago: University of Chicago Press, 1962), p. 137.

2. The Surgeons' Case (*Stratton v. Swanlond*). Year Book 48 Edw. III, pl. 11, f. 6 (Hilary Term) 1374.

3. A. K. R. Kiralfy, *A Source Book of English Law* (London: Sweet & Maxwell, 1957), pp. 185–87.

4. *Waldon* v. *Mareschal*. Year Book 43 Edw. III, pl. 38, f. 33 (Michaelmas Term) 1369.

5. Farrier's Case. Year Book 46 Edw. III, pl. 19, f. 19 (Trinity Term) 1372.

6. Kiralfy, *Source Book of English Law,* pp. 184–85.

7. Harry Thomas Riley, *Memorials of London and London Life in the Thirteenth, Fourteenth, and Fifteenth Centuries* (London: Longmans, Green, & Co., n.d.), pp. 273–74.

8. Madeleine Pelner Cosman, "Medieval Medical Malpractice: The Dicta and the Dockets," *Bull. New York Acad. Med.* 49:22–47, January 1973.

9. Riley, *Memorials of London and London Life,* p. 337.

10. *Bonham* v. *Atkins.* Eng. Rep. 123:928–33; Brownlee and Goldesborough 2:256 (1609).

11. Theodore F. T. Plucknett, "Bonham's Case and Judicial Review," *Harvard Law Rev.* 49:30–70, 1927.

12. "Dr. Bonham's Case." Reports of Sir Edward Coke Kt. 8:114–21 (London: E. and R. Nutt and R. Gosling, 1727), p. 118.

13. Lewis C. Warden, *The Life of Blackstone* (Charlottesville: Michie Co., 1938), pp. 313–48.

14. J. A. C. Grant, "The Gild Returns to America," *J. Politics* 4:303–36, August 1952, pp. 310–11; 4:458–77, November 1942.

15. Walter Gellhorn, *Individual Freedom and Governmental Restraints* (Baton Rouge: Louisiana State University Press, 1956), p. 115.

16. Grant, "The Gild Returns to America," p. 324.

17. *The People, ex rel. Gray* v. *The Medical Society of the County of Erie.* New York Rep. (Barbour) 24:570–80, 1963 (1857), pp. 570–71.

18. "Note. Malpractice and Medical Testimony," *Harvard Law Rev.* 77:333–50, 1963.

19. "Note. Overcoming the 'Conspiracy of Silence': Statutory and Common-Law Innovations," *Minnesota Law Rev.* 45:1019–50, 1961.

20. Tully Scott and Grover C. Herring, "Medical Malpractice in Florida," *U. Florida Law Rev.* 12:121–55, 1959.

21. *L'Orange* v. *The Medical Protective Company.* Federal Rep., 2d series 394:57–64, 1968.

22. *Steininga et al.* v. *Thron.* Atlantic Rep., 2d series, 105:10–12, 1954, p. 11.

23. Jon R. Walz, "The Rise and Gradual Fall of the Locality Rule in Medical Malpractice Litigation," *DePaul Law Rev.* 28:408–20, 1969.

24. Charles A. Ragan, "The Malpractice Pall Over Medicine," *Resident and Staff Physician* 20:9–10, April 1974.

25. Richard M. Marcus, "You Doctors Are Making Too Much of Malpractice," *Medical Economics* 50:174–86, 28 May 1972, p. 184.

26. Marie Lambert, "Malpractice: Unfounded Postulates." Letter to the editor, *New York Times,* 2 May 1975, p. 34.

27. Anon., "Today's Top Lawyers: They Never Had It So Good." *Medical Economics* 49:176–77; 193–92; 25 September 1972, p. 177.

28. *Niles* v. *City of San Rafael.* California Appl., 3d series 42:230–45, 1974.

29. F. B. MacKinnon, *Contingent Fees for Legal Services: A Report of the American Bar Association* (Chicago: Aldine Publishing Co., 1964), pp. 9–15, 38–39.

30. Gellhorn *Individual Freedom and Governmental Restraints,* p. 143.

31. Alexander M. Carr-Saunders, "Metropolitan Conditions and Traditional Professional Relationships," *The Metropolis in Modern Life,* ed. Robert M. Fisher (Garden City: Doubleday & Co., 1955), pp. 279–87.

THE INFLUENCE OF ABBA HILLEL SILVER ON THE EVOLUTION OF REFORM JUDAISM

LEON I. FEUER

Abba Hillel Silver, 1893–1963, was ordained at the Hebrew Union College in 1915. In 1917 he was elected to the pulpit of The Temple, Congregation Tifereth Israel, Cleveland, Ohio, which he served to the end of his life. He held the posts of President of the Central Conference of American Rabbis and of the Zionist Organization of America, Chairman of the American Zionist Emergency Council and of the Jewish Agency for Palestine, American section, in which capacity he successfully argued for the Jewish Commonwealth before the Assembly of the United Nations.

FROM its very inception in Germany as a movement within Jewish life, Reform Judaism, true to its essential genius, has been changing and developing while endeavoring to remain faithful to the fundamental spirit of the historic faith. American Reform is quite different from its German ancestor, although not as radically so as might be imagined. The handful of rabbis who wrote the Pittsburgh Platform in 1883, and even the much larger group who half a century later adopted the Columbus Platform, would not be hard put to reconcile their view of Jewish doctrine and practice with those of the majority of contemporary Reform rabbis, for there are indissoluble links between them, one being the subject of this essay. Current Reform seems to be placing greater and greater stress upon the peoplehood of Israel, upon the ethnic aspects of the ties between the various Jewish communities in the world, and upon an increasing quota of ceremony and ritual. We hear demands for the formulation of an official Reform Halacha, in the hope, probably vain, of putting the movement more in line with rabbinic tradition and thus becoming less anathema to the official Orthodoxies. There is even a trend toward accepting the claim to centrality, and therefore to primacy in the Jewish world, of the reborn State of Israel. Abba Hillel Silver would have heartily endorsed some of these changes; indeed, as we shall see, he was a significant force in effecting them. Others he would have vigorously opposed, for, believing as he did that there were certain vitally basic themes running through Jewish thought and experience, he would regard them, as we shall see, as somewhat of a departure from the mainstream.

From a detached, objective historical perspective, no single cause, and certainly no one person, can be credited with bringing about the transformations which have been and are taking place within American Reform. The influx of East European immigrants from the 1880s on produced, in its second- and third-generation wake, an infusion into the primarily German Jewish composition of our Reform congregations, a type of membership and lay leadership nostalgically conditioned toward the introduction of traditional practices in public worship, such as Bar and Bat Mitzvah, and into home family observance of the Sabbath Eve Kiddush and the kindling of Sabbath and Chanukah lights. On the Eastern seaboard, where the impact was more immediate, it was the rule rather than the exception for Reform congregations to employ cantors, and it was not uncommon for the worshippers to wear hats and talethim. In fact, some congregations had never departed from these more traditional usages. In the Midwest, where German influence remained stronger for some time, Reform went to greater lengths in eliminating vestiges of Orthodox practice, in some instances going to such extremes—one such congregation ironically being Tifereth Israel of Cleveland, which was to be Silver's pulpit—as ending the regular Sabbath cycle of Torah readings. These congregations have been rapidly catching up with the procession of change. The process has, of course, been intensively accelerated by such epoch-shaking events as the Holocaust and the rebirth of Israel, which have pushed to the foreground of Jewish consciousness the desire for demonstrating in every possible form, including religious symbolism, the closing of ranks and the cohesiveness of Jewish brotherhood the world over.

While giving due consideration to the influence of these historic causes in producing change in American Reform, one would be less than faithful to a spiritual heritage which gave us an Abraham, a Moses, a David, the prophets, and some of the eminent rabbinic personalities, if one did not make due allowance for the contributions of individual personalities. After all, Reform did and still does bear the indelible stamp of the results of the labors of Isaac Mayer Wise, without whose vision and far-ranging organizational capacities the movement, and its subsidiary institutions, the College, the Union, and the Central Conference, might not as soon or perhaps ever have come into being. It is the thesis of this study that perhaps equal with Wise, and certainly second only to him, American Reform thought and practice owe much of their configuration to another powerful personality, the late Abba Hillel Silver. The influence of Silver, as we shall note, was both diffuse and intensely concentrated. He entered the Hebrew Union College in 1911 and graduated in 1915. He came from a background of rabbinic ancestry. He received a thorough training in biblical and rabbinic lore. Apt quotations from the sources sprang readily to his lips. In a period which was witnessing the revival of Hebrew as a living tongue, he was fluent in its usage. In New York's Lower East Side, he had been an active leader in the strongly Zionist- and Hebrew-oriented Herzl Zion Club, which gave both to the rabbinate and to Zionist leadership a number of noted personalities. In 1917 he became the rabbi of The Temple, Cleveland, Ohio-Congregation Tifereth Israel, then one of the most prominent and radically Reform congregations in the United States. Under his leadership it became not only one of the largest congregations in the country, but a pioneer in the Jewish and Hebrew education of its children. He is said to have inspired, helped to train and sponsor more candidates for the rabbinate, including his own son and the present writer, than any other alumnus of the Hebrew Union College. The chief source of his influence, however, is to be found in the innumerable addresses and learned papers he was called upon to deliver at the College and before gatherings of the Central Conference of American Rabbis and the Union of American Hebrew Congregations. His published works, usually popular in presentation although authoritative in learning, enjoyed wide readership. On the occasion of the celebration by his congregation of his sixtieth birthday and the thirty-fifth anniversary of his incumbency, the writer, representing the Central Conference of American Rabbis, said:

So highlighted with drama has been Dr. Silver's leadership in the rescue and national renaissance of our people, that it is easy to overlook his equally significant leadership of the religious life of American Jewry. During these past thirty-five years profound changes have been taking place in our Reform movement. Demonstrating once again Judaism's amazing capacity for adjustment, Reform has been evolving into a logical and coherent synthesis of the best of our traditional ideas and practices with the American way of life, and thus becoming the pattern of the future for the whole of American Jewry. My use of the figure thirty-five is not fortuitous. It parallels the period of Dr. Silver's rabbinate in this congregation. For he has emerged during this period as the single most potent force in shaping the form and guiding the direction which Judaism is likely to take in this country. Retrospectively analyzed, his books, his papers and addresses before the Central Conference of American Rabbis, at the College and before other groups will be seen to constitute the text and guidebook of that development. At the same time, The Temple, its school and its organizational program have been the laboratory in which his ideas have been tested and found valid. With an uncanny instinct for what is basically and integrally Jewish, his thinking has represented that balance and fusion of the universal and the particular, the Messianic and the nationalist, the prophetic and priestly strains which constitute historic Judaism correctly understood. An uncompromising fighter for the political independence of Israel, he continued to insist that religion is the primary vocation and function of the Jewish people.

That judgment seems to be as accurate today as when it was first pronounced.

The first and, of course, the most obvious impact which Silver made upon Reform ideology was to wean it away from its anti-Zionist, anti-nationalist stance. This was an effort which began very early in his rabbinical career. This he helped to effect not only by his own activism in the Zionist movement and leadership in the effort to bring about the establishment of the Jewish State, but by his creative and successful synthesis of Reform theology with the nationalist philosophy of Jewish life. It was by all odds, as we shall see, a master stroke. It now seems passing strange, with the preponderant majority of rabbis enthusiastically pro-Israel, sponsoring pilgrimages to Eretz of adults and children; with the Central Conference of American Rabbis holding conventions there; with the Union of American Hebrew Congregations sponsoring the growth of liberal congregations and schools there; with the World Union of Progressive Judaism establishing its headquarters in Jerusalem; with Reform laymen in the vanguard of financial support for the state: to think of the movement as having been adamantly and often bitterly opposed to the Zionist idea. Just a half century or so ago, although not in itself an official document, the Pittsburgh Platform voiced the more or less generally accepted position of Reform Zionism. The phrasing is worth recalling.

We recognize in the modern era of universal culture of heart and intellect the approaching of the realization of Israel's great Messianic hope for the establishment of the Kingdom of truth, justice and peace among all men. We consider ourselves no longer a nation, but a religious community and therefore expect neither a return to Palestine, nor sacrificial mission under the sons of Aaron, nor the restoration of any of the laws concerning the Jewish State.

Central to Reform doctrine of the time was the idea of the Mission of Israel, that is, the divinely appointed assignment to the Jewish people to work for the realization of a Messianic Age upon earth. In his introductory essay to *Reform Judaism: A Book of Essays by Alumni of the Hebrew Union College*, Dr. Bernard J. Bamberger wrote: "Stress was laid [by the early reformers] on the prophetic doctrine that Israel was God's Messenger, bringing the doctrine of righteousness to mankind, so the Messianic hope of universal brotherhood and the Mission of Israel emerged as Reform's major concepts next to its doctrine about the Oneness of God." Silver accepted the idea of the Mission as central not only to Reform but to historic Jewish thought. It will be fascinating to see how he employs it to reorient Reform's posture toward Zionism.

Although it is clear that from the beginning of his rabbinate he made it a primary aim to effect a shift in Reform Judaism's posture from anti- to pro-Zionism, he felt that the groundwork for such an effort had to be carefully and cautiously laid. He clearly did not believe in sledgehammer methods. There is a fascinating set of correspondence in the Silver Memorial Archives (located in The Temple, Cleveland, Ohio) which documents his strategy. Although the subject was to agitate its discussions again and again, the Central Conference of American Rabbis had adopted a resolution which seemed to express the majority view. The first sentence read: "We totally disapprove of any attempt for the establishment of a Jewish State." This was in reaction to the Basle Program adopted by the World Zionist Organization under the leadership of Theodor Herzl. In 1916, one year after he entered the CCAR, Silver participated in a symposium in which he said rather mildly that the rabbis must come to understand "Nationalism, Political or Cultural Zionism, the renaissance of Hebrew or Yiddish literature, the aesthetic revival—valuable in so far as they intensify Jewish communal life—as so many more dikes against the onrushing tides of assimilation—.'' In 1917 Great Britain issued the Balfour Declaration and received the mandate for Palestine, thus setting in motion greatly increased activity in the Jewish world toward the colonization and economic development of the country. In 1920 Silver joined with Max Heller, Martin Meyer, and Stephen Wise in requesting the Central Conference of American Rabbis, in view of the mandate, to discuss the role it could play in the upbuilding of Jewish Palestine. In a letter to Wise, he expressed skepticism about the results to be achieved by it, fearing at that point that Conference action would either be negative or so tame as to defeat the purpose. Nothing tangible apparently came of it. In 1921 he wrote to the then President of the Conference, Dr. Edward N. Calisch, requesting cooperation with the nonpolitical Palestine Development Council. Dr. Calisch replied indicating approval of the Executive Board with the proviso that there be equal representation of Zionists and non-Zionists in the Council. Obviously there was still considerable hesitancy about the possible political implications of CCAR involvement even in nonpolitical activity. Later, replying to a letter from Rabbi James G. Heller suggesting an organization of Reform and Conservative Zionist rabbis to work for common objectives, Silver responded significantly, ''I am not in favor of organizing Zionist members in the Conservative and Reform Wings as a unit. I believe it is poor tactics to say the least. Our objectives should be not to divide the American rabbinate into two sharply distinguished and opposite groups but *in winning control* over all existing rabbinical organizations for Zionist purposes.'' Written in 1930, this letter expresses confidence that such control can be won. Prophetic in view of the later appearance upon the scene of the troublesome American Council for Judaism, he feared that organizing Zionist rabbis would provoke the organization of anti-Zionist rabbis and mean an embitterment of the Zionist controversy. A few years later, when he was in the President's chair, Heller assented to the introduction and passage of a resolution favoring the establishment of a Jewish army to participate in World War II. Arguing that this violated the posture of neutrality on the Zionist issue upon which the Conference had by this time agreed, and that the resolution was therefore out of order, the anti-Zionists did precisely what Silver warned might happen. They tried to split the Conference and Reform Judaism by convoking a meeting in Atlantic City with their lay followers to organize the American Council on Judaism. By 1937 the Pittsburgh Platform was considered both inadequate and outdated, and was replaced by the "Guiding Principles" adopted by the Conference in Columbus, Ohio (popularly known as the Columbus Platform), with Silver, a member of the committee which formulated them, arguing persuasively in their favor. In this document, greater weight is given to ceremonial observance. The major changes, however, were the emphasis upon the tie between Reform and world Jewry, and upon the redevelopment of Palestine. "In the rehabilitation of Palestine, the land hallowed by memories and hopes, we behold the promise of renewed life for many of our brethren. We affirm the obligation of all Jewry to aid in its upbuilding as a Jewish homeland by endeavoring to make it not only a haven of refuge for the oppressed but also a center of Jewish culture and spiritual life." By this time both the Conference and the Union of American Hebrew Congregations had revoked their anti-Zionist resolutions and become officially neutral on the subject of Political Zionism. Silver was satisfied with this measure of progress, eminently confident that history would take care of the rest, at least as far as practical steps were concerned, toward winning Reform Judaism over to a favorable, even a supportive, stance toward a political solution of the Jewish problem. In this somewhat uncharacteristic go-slow approach, and by his refusal in the early stages to support measures which might rend apart the institutions of Reform, he demonstrated not only his own statesmanship and keen political sense of what was possible, but his earnest view that while perhaps not as urgently immediate a cause as Zionism, of which he became the undisputed leader in the United States, Reform as an idea and a movement was important and precious to him.

He had a larger goal to which he was committed and to which

he devoted much of his thinking and writing. His aim was to demonstrate doctrinally that Zionism and Reform not only were not incompatible but that they were complementary and essential one to the other. Many of his major papers and addresses delivered before the Central Conference of American Rabbis, the Union of American Hebrew Congregations, at the Hebrew Union College, and elsewhere are devoted to establishing this synthesis. Since no one was in greater demand as a speaker before audiences of laymen, many thousands of whom must have listened to him over and over; and since his presentations were characterized not only by his matchlessly persuasive oratory and analytical power, but by his mastery both of the sources and of Jewish historical knowledge, taken together these facts fully justify the description of him as a major influence in the shaping of contemporary Reform thought. It is fascinating to study the design of the ideological structure which Dr. Silver was rearing.

He begins with a critique of the anti-Zionist orientation of the early reformers while at the same time accepting the basic assumptions which they postulated for the movement. His criticism—and it is never the carping or sneering kind which one finds so frequently not only among the opponents of Reform but within our own ranks—takes several forms. He points out that the founders of the movement, products of the buoyant and often uncritical liberalism of the nineteenth century, regarded progress as a steady, uninterrupted advance, instead of a cyclical movement which each time results only in a slight gain for mankind. It is a recurring note in Silver's thinking that while the Messianic hope remains constant, one must be realistic in the expectation, the timetable of its coming. He also makes an interesting distinction between "reform" and "modernize." The reformers were too eager to modernize, whereas true Reform, he maintains, breaks with the present as well as with the past, attempting to restore religion to its timeless spiritual essence. Prophetic and later Pharisaic Judaism, he points out, never wanted Israel to be like but unlike the other nations. They opposed conformity to the pagan and heathen world of their time. He was, of course, severely critical of the reformers' attempt to separate Judaism from the sense of peoplehood and nationalism which had always been indispensable elements in Jewish survival. Judaism tried to maintain a sensible balance between nationalism and internationalism. In "The World Crisis and Jewish Survival" he argues that the anti-national pronouncements of the American reformers were an import from German Reform, made not out of any great prophetic universal impulse but to protect Jewish rights of citizenship by making the proper impression on the civil authorities. They seemed to believe that the solution for anti-Semitism was to eradicate all manifestations of separatism. For some Jews this meant total assimilation, for others the purging of all nationalist elements from Jewish thought. The result, as in the case of the Mendelssohn family, was conversion to Christianity. Neither in Germany nor in France did assimilationist tendencies avert anti-Semitism. The same tendencies operated in Russia, but there the Jews, with Leo Pinsker and his *Autoemancipation* as forerunner, set about solving their problems through self-help and more especially through national concentration and cultural survival. The appeasing patriotism of the anti-nationalists was useless because it completely ignored the lessons, the bitterly learned lessons, of our history. Jewish political emancipation, where it grudgingly occurred in Western Europe, and anti-Semitism were parallel movements, just as the Inquisition and Ghetto paralleled the Renaissance and Reformation. Whenever gains seemed to be made toward granting Jews civil rights, the forces of bigotry returned to the attack again and again. The basic problem of homelessness, which made the Jew vulnerable, remained unsolved. To drive home this point, Silver uses a striking figure of speech: "Our virtuosity is wasted on a stringless fiddle."

Silver did not hesitate to attack the position of the early reformers at their strongest point, the keystone of Reform thought, the Mission idea, not as others have done by denying its validity, but by affirming it, making it the heart of his own system, and insisting that it was entirely compatible with nationalism. His most important statement on this subject is to be found in that remarkable symposium on "Israel" before the 1935 meeting of the Central Conference of American Rabbis. It was this address which may be said to have made the greatest intellectual impact in effecting the shift of Reform Judaism from an anti- to a pro-Zionist position. In it he reminds us that the idea of a universal mission for Israel is exilic. It does not appear in pre-exilic Scripture. It was meant to give the dispersed nation a sense of dignity and worth. It was not meant as a substitute for national existence, but as an addition, a bulwark. The prophets who preached mission, like Second Isaiah, also proclaimed restoration. He quotes from Isaiah 43 (5–6): "I will bring thy seed from the east and will gather thee from the west. I will say to the North: 'Give up' and to the South, 'Keep not back; bring thy sons from afar and My daughters from the ends of the earth.' " Centuries later the same note is struck by Judah Ha-Levi, who closes his *Cuzari* by comparing Israel to the heart among the nations, which must return to its own land and revive its language if the gift of prophecy is to live. Judaism always tried to maintain this balance between nationalism and inter-nationalism, between preserving its identity and devoting itself to universal goals. It had room for all sects and points of view except Christianity, which under the leadership of Paul became anti-national. Paul saw all nations, including Israel, vanishing into universal anonymity. The early American Reform rabbis saved this fate only for Israel. Thus Silver saw Reform opposition to nationalism as more Paulinian Christian than Jewish. But even the reformers had to resort to the term "people" because they could not find a more suitable or accurate definition. Indeed, Kaufmann Kohler, who convoked the meeting which produced the Pittsburgh Platform, used a racial definition of Judaism. Jews, he declared, are born into the status of being Jewish. Silver concludes his trenchant analysis of the meaning of Israel by suggesting that although Judaism is the crowning achievement of the Jewish people, the people is transcendent to it as is the artist to his creation.

Thus Silver saw no conflict between his Zionism and Reform

Judaism's insistence on the Covenant-Mission with its Messianic expectations as being the very heart of Jewish thought. Throughout his active career he constantly strove—and one may say successfully—for a synthesis between them. He contended that the establishment of the Jewish State would more effectively serve the aims of the Mission, because it would help safeguard the integrity of a people contending everywhere in the Diaspora with the forces of assimilation. There could be no Mission without a strong, secure people to exemplify, to practice, and to teach it. "Liberal Judaism has slowly disentangled itself from the meshes of an anti-nationalist dogma in which it was caught in the early years of its development and which was never an essential part of its teaching." Perhaps his best formulation of the synthesis of the Mission ideal with the Peoplehood of Israel and the national aspirations of the Jewish people occurs in that remarkable essay, "The Democratic Impulse in Jewish History," based on his conference lecture before the 1928 convention of the rabbis. The date is significant. It comes relatively early in his rabbinical career, and demonstrates that he was in the process of formulating a clear, consistent philosophy of Jewish life which would combine his Zionist convictions with his interpretation of Liberal Judaism. In it he stresses the universalism of the Pharisees—he tends to see all of Jewish history as a kind of tension and struggle between Pharisaic and Sadducean attitudes—who were devotees of the Covenant-Mission and at the same time fervent nationalists. They sought to preserve both the Covenant and the people of the Covenant, both the soul of the race and its body. "Liberal Judaism placed itself in direct line of descent from this prophetic-Pharisaic tradition where it accepted as focal in its ideology the Mission of Israel." He goes on to assert that Reform, in correctly holding fast to the Covenant and to the Mission ideal, erred in assuming that it was no longer necessary to stress the national ideal and to maintain strong group discipline. Anticipating the line of argument he was later to pursue in the symposium on "Israel," he suggests that Reform, like early Christianity, imagined the Messianic Age was at hand.

He describes this as the religious romanticism of the early reformers and their prime error. They were correct about the Mission, but they failed to evolve a program by which the people would be constantly reminded that they are a "peculiar, covenanted and consecrated people" and through which they would be saved from assimilation. Although politically a Herzlian Zionist, he interprets the spiritual Zionism of Ahad Ha-Am as a form of the Mission concept. The Exile may have temporarily discredited the Mission because Israel appeared in the world's eyes as the defeated people of a defeated God. Therefore it is only the national restoration which will provide the dignity and spiritual renewal which can provide a needed impetus to the Mission, and then he quotes Ezekiel: "It is not for your sake that I am about to act, O household of Israel, but for My holy name. When I restore My holiness in their sight through My dealings with you, the nations shall know that I am the Lord."

With the Zionist objective attained through the establishment of Israel, Dr. Silver turned his attention to the problems of the future, especially those relating to the relationship between the new Jewish State and the Diaspora; the prospects of Jewish communities living outside Israel, and especially of American Jewry. He approached his discussion of these matters with his usual realism, logic, and common sense. Perhaps the best place to begin is with the address he delivered in 1948 before the Biennial of the Union of American Hebrew Congregations, shortly after the founding of the state. In it he declares his hope that the establishment of Israel will put an end to the concepts of Galut and of the Wandering Jew. The Jew will fight for his rights with more confidence and resolution. How accurate that prediction turned out is well attested by the recent events in the Soviet Union, where many Jews are indeed demonstrating a remarkable kind of Jewish pride and courage. He believed that the Jewish population of Israel would reach three to four million, making it the largest center of Jewish life outside the United States. That now seems readily attainable. "Life in Israel will be characterized, I believe, by that same energy, initiative and inventiveness which have characterized American life." The Diaspora will continue, just as there was a Diaspora prior to 70 C.E., and will, as then, have the majority of Jews. There was no question of dual allegiance then, and there is none now. Jerusalem was their religious center. They made pilgrimages there and contributed to the support of the Temple. In our time Israel will be the nonpolitical center of the nation, and Jews will support and aid in its development. A by-product of the establishment of Israel will be the end of the Zionist, anti-Zionist debate. He goes on to discuss the effects of the establishment of the state on the Diaspora and the prediction of rapid assimilation. He denied that this will be or need be the outcome, pointing to the ancient Diaspora, where there were assimilationist tendencies, but yet the great majority remained loyal. They carried on widespread proselytizing activity. The Jews of Babylon produced the Babylonian Talmud. Silver was never one, however, to engage in overoptimistic or wishful thinking. He warned that we cannot be certain of Diaspora survival any more than we can be certain of democracy. Everything depends upon the means we employ to strengthen it. American Jewry, he hoped, would ultimately be able to divert its resources to its own strengthening. Indeed, we now find increasing demands upon Jewish Federations to devote larger proportions of their funds for Jewish education. In this connection, his comment is significant. "We are constrained to acknowledge that the thin wafer, the melba toast type of Jewish education which our children receive in our Sunday Schools, is not the kind of a spiritual and cultural diet which can nourish and sustain a vigorous Jewish life, and one which does not promise well for the future."

Silver did not claim for himself any expertise in the field of Jewish education and only rarely wrote on or addressed himself to the subject. Nevertheless, he was deeply interested in its progress and scrupulously followed the developments in his own school at The Temple in Cleveland, frequently visiting its classrooms and making suggestions and critical comments to its supervisors and teachers. He had, however, a definite philosophy of and ideas about Jewish education. He was skeptical about newfangled methods and too frequent experimentation, believing that the basic goals would be lost sight of. He was contemptuous of theories which would make the Jewish classroom a place of entertainment, designed to help children to grow up into ''happy Jews.'' For him, Judaism was a serious business, and he wanted children to be inculcated with the seriousness of it. He advocated the tried and tested techniques of Jewish religious life—learning, study, contemplation, prayer, and observance. Few or many does not matter—old or new—what matters is *Kavanah*—Intent. He contended that Torah is the basis of all Jewish education. Jews were not great philosophers. For them *Chochmah* (wisdom) is derived from Torah. ''Jewish Education,'' he said in an address before the Jewish Education Committee, ''was an experience in and preparation for modern living in the sight of God. Its basis is the Bible and its rabbinic derivatives and its locale is the Synagog.'' While it was impossible to trace a direct opinion on the subject, one may infer from that last phrase and from his well-known strong views on the separation of Church and State that he would not have been favorably disposed to, although he might not have opposed, the present trend toward the growth of Jewish parochial schools. He often indicated that it was not the amount of time spent in Jewish education which mattered as much as the manner in which the time was utilized.

In one area of Jewish education, however, he had, and frequently expressed, emphatically positive views, the study of the Hebrew language. Himself intimate with the Hebrew sources and eloquent in spoken Hebrew, he insisted that the language was the vital core of the curriculum of every Jewish school. The Temple was among the earliest of the large Reform congregations, if not the very first, to make Hebrew a compulsory subject of instruction. Speaking in 1950 to the Central Conference on ''The Future of the American Jewish Community,'' he said this: ''No Jewish community ever contributed culturally or scholastically to Jewish life which did not favor the Hebrew language and literature. No Jewish community ever survived for long which ignored Hebrew. This is an ineluctable fact of our existence—we have armor against everything except 'Am Harazut.' " He goes on to point to the great creative Jewish communities of the past and to the fact of their deliberate and extensive cultivation of the Hebrew language and literature. As in the case of other classical languages, the rediscovery of Hebrew affected the progress of Jewish life. This was evident both in the Haskalah movement and in the birth of modern Zionism. Hebrew has been second only to the Torah. Hebrew will always be the basic bond between Israel and the communities outside. Here he employs one of his characteristically trenchant phrases. "If American Jewry are not careful they are likely to lie down with integration and rise up with assimilation," and concludes his discussion with the rabbinic dictum, "As soon as a child can speak, his father should teach him the Shema, Torah, and the sacred tongue." It is not to be doubted that Silver's reiterated advocacy must be counted a significant factor in the now widespread study of the language in Reform congregations, a tendency, of course, latterly accelerated by the rebirth of Israel and the visits there of thousands of young people.

Despite the enormous investment of time and energy, a lifetime singularly devoted to Zionist activity and leadership, and the achievement of national independence for the Jewish people, it nevertheless remains the fact that Abba Hillel Silver did not regard Israel as the be-all and end-all of Jewish destiny, a view now becoming quite fashionable among Sammy-come-latelies to the Zionist movement, bandwagon hoppers, many of whom were at one time not only indifferent but bitterly hostile opponents of Zionism. Here again his finely balanced view of history asserted itself. The establishment of Israel was for him not the final act in the drama of universal salvation, but an essential step. Zionism was more, much more, than a secular political movement, although it had to use secular tools for its realization. He contended that the foundations of the state were laid long ago in the persevering Messianic hopes, the longing and prayers of one people "which enswathed its life as an element." To put it differently, his was a larger view which saw Zionism as one of the instrumentalities which the Jewish people would utilize in order to carry forward its universal mission. He was critical of what he called "Pinsker Canaanites," who think that nationalism is the culmination of Jewish existence and striving, and who therefore negate the Diaspora. He foresaw the disappearance of this attitude. He probably would have regarded the current discussion about whether Israel should be regarded as central and primary in the Jewish world as largely academic. While Israel can be a source of support to the Diaspora, we in the Jewish communities outside the land will have to supply our own nourishment. "We cannot survive on borrowed rations." He believed firmly in the unity and integrity of the Jewish people, the solidarity of Israel both in and out of the land, both Israel and the Diaspora being equally essential to the future, both the Mission and the national life which helped to secure the survival of the people of the Mission. More of this later. It is interesting to note that he approvingly quoted Ahad Ha-Am's statement: "The salvation of Israel will come to pass through prophets and not through diplomats." Also worth noting is that he warned against the development in Israel of a fanatical clericalism which resists cooperation with other Jewish religious bodies. He admonished Orthodox groups to learn that in a free country religion cannot be enforced by fiat. He was also convinced that liberal Judaism will be needed in Israel. Young people in Israel now get their spiritual discipline from the motivations of building and defending the state. When that period is over they will need spiritual motivation, and it can only come from Judaism. Reform Judaism, however, cannot be imported into Israel. A liberal Judaism can and will evolve there which will be responsive to its own special environment.

It is the view of this writer, easily substantiated by a survey of Silver's ideas, not only that Silver must be placed in the mainstream of classic Reform thought, but that, along with Isaac M. Wise, he was a truly major factor in shaping the thinking of American Reform. This may be surprising to those who were aware of his zealous Zionism and who have thought of him primarily as a Zionist leader and spokesman. It is nevertheless true. Primarily he thought of himself as a Reform rabbi. In his last public appearance before the Central Conference in 1963 shortly before his death, he said this in a dialogue with his classmate and friend, Dr. Solomon B. Freehof: ''Zionism has always been a part of my conception of historic Judaism, and I came to it not as a secular nationalist, but as a devout Jew, and I never permitted my Zionist activities to push aside or to overshadow my activities and duties as a rabbi.'' In his introduction to *Reform Judaism*, previously adverted to, Dr. Bernard J. Bamberger says that Wise made a movement out of American Reform, a distinct movement in which he tried to combine American and Jewish values. In this sense Silver may be said to have followed the Wise tradition. One cannot be familiar with his many sermons and addresses on public themes without realizing that he was deeply immersed both in Jewish historic values and in the American democratic spirit, bolstering his view on the latter out of the immense store of his knowledge of the former. He clearly understood the essence of Reform, once defining its contributions as the substitution of scholarship for scholasticism, of liberty for authority, and the reinterpretation in modern terms of the ancient doctrine of the Mission of Israel. It is fascinating to note his apologia for Wise in his Founder's Day address delivered in 1950 at the Hebrew Union College. He points to Wise's insistence upon an informed and learned rabbinate and laity. While expressing regret that so much of the energies of the early reformers, believing that the universal age was at hand, was spent in opposing Zionism, he went on to point out that when Isaac M. Wise spoke of universal religion, he did not mean a general fusion of faiths, he meant Judaism and the conversion of the world to Jewish ideals. He then spoke approvingly of Wise's vision of the United States as a perfectly Jewish state and under a Jewish government in the strictest sense of Moses. Homiletical hyperbole! Perhaps. One can imagine that he would not have found himself in disagreement with one of the very radical German reformers, Samuel Holdheim:

Judaism wants to purify the language of the nations, but to leave to each people its own tongue. It wishes for one heart and one soul, but not for one sound and one tone. It does not wish to destroy the particular characteristics of the nations. It does not wish to stultify the direction of spirit and sentiment which their history has brought forth. It does not wish that all should be absorbed and encompassed by the characteristics of the Jewish people. Least of all does it wish to extinguish the characteristics of the Jewish people and to eliminate those expressions of the living spirit which were created through the union and spirit of the Jewish faith. (Quoted from Plaut, *The Rise of Reform Judaism*.)

More significantly, what puts Silver in the direct line of Reform ideology was his insistence that religion, Judaism—note, not nationalism—is and must be the central factor in Jewish existence. There can, of course, be no effective religion without peoplehood integrated by racial, religious, and historical ties and possessing common memories, traditions, loyalties, aspirations, and holding one language, Hebrew, sacred, but of all these elements religion remains the most important. In a very significant paper, "Religion in Present Day Jewish Life," read in 1939 at the Biennial of the Union of American Hebrew Congregations, he pointed to the disasters of the twentieth century, including those which overtook Jewish life, and goes on to say, "What has been tragically missing in our civilization has been the compelling and coordinating belief in the great human goals which religion and religion alone, has set for mankind." He argued that there are no substitutes in Jewish life for religion, neither philanthropy nor culture nor nationalism. (How strange for such an ardent Zionist!) " . . . The pattern must be Judaism, the Judaism of the Torah, the Synagogue and the prayer book." He goes on to suggest that while Jewish education should be nationalist in sympathy and linguistic, it should be primarily religious and ethical in content and direction. The upbuilding of Palestine (this is, of course, prior to the event of the Restoration) and the maintenance of Jewish religious life in America and elsewhere are not opposing goals or substitutes for each other.

Silver supported his view of religion as primary in Judaism

with his uncompromising theism. He once counseled newly ordained rabbis not to be ashamed to speak about God. He reminded us that many believed mankind could dispense with Israel's faith and code and could achieve freedom, justice, dignity, courage, brotherhood, and peace without reference to God and the techniques of religion. But they achieved—in his words—only dictatorship, slavery, littleness of stature, fear, hate, and war. They put their hope not in spiritual conversion, not in moral regeneration, but in a precipitous scientific and intellectual progress which has now hauled rider, horse, and chariot alike into one bloody and ruinous tangle. Here he employed one of those remarkably terse statements charged with meaning. "There is never any forward movement in Society without an inward movement in man." Elsewhere he pointed to the fact that when God is dethroned, a false god takes his place, and when men reject the sanctification of life, it becomes cheapened and the individual is reduced to a statistic. Prophetic, is this not? Generally rationalist in his approach to questions, he was not above adding a touch of mysticism to his discussions of God and religion. As the result of the modern Jewish tragedy, he foresaw a new surge of mysticism in Jewish thought. The resurgence of interest in Hasidism and the popularity of the writings of Elie Wiesel would certainly seem to bear this out. He himself spoke of Messianism as the redemption of Israel, leading to the redemption of the world, this being one of his earlier contributions to Reform thought, in which he interwove his nationalism with his view of the Mission.

As we might expect, he was contemptuous of Jewish secularists. Carrying out his Pharisee-Sadducee analogy, to which we have already referred, he denounced Jewish secularists as "modern Sadducees" and referred to himself as a modern Pharisee. "The modern Pharisees will proceed to enrich and beautify and vitalize Jewish group life. They will hold fast to all the agencies which in the past preserved the integrity of the people—Israel's language, Israel's love and Israel's hope of national rehabilitation, Israel's memory laden customs and habits of life adjusted to modern needs." He is critical not only of the secularists, who have abandoned the centrality of religion, but of the so-called Jewish culturalists. "But one wonders what the distinctiveness of Jewish culture is if it is not in the dynamics of prophecy, the passionate outreaching for Malchut Shamayim (The Kingdom of God)." If the Jew decides to assimilate, it will be because he is ready to abandon his faith, and "no quantum of Jewish music and Jewish art or books on Jewish literature and philosophy will be potent enough to save him." Taking into account his view of the centrality of the Mission concept, which they have officially abandoned, although close scrutiny will reveal that this is really not so, this may be taken as a clear attack on the Reconstructionist movement. It may be assumed that he would have taken the same position toward those Jewish survivalists today who believe that an attachment to the purely ethnic elements in Jewish life is sufficient.

It is interesting to speculate about what Silver's attitude would have been toward the recent trend in Reform toward more ceremonialism; what he would have made of Reform rabbis wearing talethim and kipahs, of bearded and hatted students at the Hebrew Union College–Jewish Institute of Religion who daven in the mornings and insist upon kosher food for their meals; what his judgment would have been of Bar and Bat Mitzvah ceremonies in Reform congregations so numerous that they have become more of a fad than anything else, with parents less concerned with their offspring's mastery of Torah than with the social success of the events. The answer is clear. He would have been very skeptical, although it is unlikely that he would have actively opposed any usage that might meaningfully enrich Jewish family or congregational observance. Although The Temple in Cleveland conducted both early Sabbath Eve and regular Saturday morning services, he continued the Sunday morning service, which provided his best means of reaching a large audience. He reminded us that Jews can pray on any day of the week. We know he was opposed to the introduction of Bar Mitzvah on the dual grounds that it would detract from the Confirmation Service and would provide youngsters with a tempting excuse for terminating their

Jewish religious education. He apparently had little faith in the multiplication of ritual practices per se. "Today it is no longer a question of more ceremonies or of fewer ceremonies, or of going backward or going forward in things external, but of going inward." He urged increased study and learning, emphasis upon the disciplines of the devotional and ethical life, in this connection calling attention to the contributions of Hasidism in its mystical concepts—*hithlahavut,* enthusiasm—*hishtapchut ha-nefesh,* outpouring of one's soul—the Tzadik as an inspired spiritual leader. Nor did he care much for the theological novelties, Existentialism, Buberism, and such, believing that whatever insights they offered were already inherent in biblical and historic Jewish concepts—God, Covenant, Prophecy, Mission, Messianism, and Israel as an eternal people. These were the material of his convictions and preaching, with especial emphasis upon prophecy, an emphasis which makes ever clearer the depth of his position as a Reform rabbi. In a prefatory note which serves quite properly as an introduction to the second volume of his published addresses, he offered this superb tribute to Israel's prophetic message:

> The good way is not through the courts of a Temple and bringing a multitude of vain offerings to God. It is not to listen to the voice of priest or prophet as if he were bringing a love song with a beautiful voice, playing well on an instrument, listening to what he says but doing nothing about it. The good way leads directly and humbly to where men persistently and prayerfully wash the blood of sin, cruelty and oppression from their hands, search, and make themselves inwardly clean, cease to do evil and learn to do good. The good way leads to where men, in struggle and in joy, build the good Society through unity, freedom and compassion. The good way is the way of the unvaried moral effort and unremitting action. At the heart of the message of Hebrew prophecy and subsequently of Judaism itself, is a summons to men not to rest content with the evils of Society or with their own personal shortcomings, but to set to work to correct them.

Abba Hillel Silver was a giant in his generation, and in this age of changing congregational and community relationships, the greatest and perhaps the last of a species. It is quite possible that we shall not see his like again. A political leader with an uncanny sense of tactics and iron nerve, a peerless orator, an overshadowing and awesome personality, a learned Jew, he was at the same time unquestionably the most brilliant advocate, the ablest spokesman, which the American Reform movement has produced in the more than a century of its history in this country.

NOTE

The material upon which this essay is based was drawn from Dr. Silver's various published works; from the *Yearbooks* of the Central Conference of American Rabbis; *Reform Judaism: Essays by HUC Alumni*; Plaut's *The History of Reform Judaism*; and the Silver Memorial Archives, The Temple, Cleveland, Ohio. The author wishes to acknowledge his indebtedness to Miss Miriam Leikind, Librarian of The Temple, for her invaluable assistance.

IGNORANCE:
THE MOTIVATION FOR
UNDERSTANDING

NORMAN HACKERMAN

Is consideration of such a topic in a Festschrift honoring a wise and good man a mockery? Not at all, because wisdom should not be looked on as the antithesis of ignorance, but rather as a synthesis from what once was ignorance. Wisdom is the stuff and essence of ignorance, since searching ignorance leads to wisdom.

We have long looked at what we know and appear to understand and have snug hosannas to man's wondrous gift, intelligence. But by any measure the ignorance of man must still be colossal, indeed, essentially constant over all of our history. We certainly do not have anything but a fragmentary grasp of nature and its fluxes, and our insight into man and mankind is even more fragmentary. The wisest among us surely understands this best.

It may well be that appreciation of the recognition of ignorance as the driving force is the best basis for acceptance of articles of faith as well as for inquisitive acquisition of fuller understanding. Awareness of ignorance leads to religious belief in its best and least formal sense, as well as to human creativity, whether it be philosophic, scientific, or artistic.

Levi Olan, speaking about how a better knowledge of physics

and chemistry does not alone reveal more about life processes, in *New Resources for Liberal Faith* (1962), said,

> Survival, then, depends upon a new emergent, which cannot be predicted in advance. It is this view of the universe, one with infinite possibilities, which renders obsolete all deterministic and mechanical descriptions of reality. Nature, it appears, has in it an infinity of different kinds of things, an unlimited variety of additional properties or qualities. There is almost no limit to the new emergents which can arise, and in time the universe will reveal an inexhaustible variety and diversity of them, totally different in quality from anything that has ever been.

Awe at our lack of understanding rather than awe at our extent of knowing has been a constantly recurring refrain for philosophers from earliest times. Socrates is said to have insisted, "I know nothing"—certainly not false modesty or an unawareness of his own talent, but a factual statement of his knowledge in relation to the vast unknown.

The point is not that it is necessary to learn humility rather than arrogance. Each of us has from time to time been depressed by his own lack of insight. Rather, the point is that it is necessary to hold in prominent view not only the advances in worthy thought and act, but also the concept of "constant of ignorance."

It probably requires reiteration that it is not ignorance itself which has value; but that it is the realization of ignorance which constitutes the driving force. This was Socrates' point in saying "I know nothing." He was asserting that he was the better for his recognition of this fact. This is one of the better antidotes to tunnel-vision fanatic positions and to the continuous disorientation of quasi-cultures. It is the flux which inhibits stagnation of the mind. It is not an exercise in modesty.

The combination of ignorance and wonder is a thread which runs through philosophy. Martin Heidegger, in *Introduction to Metaphysics*, writes,

> In the commonsense view, to be sure, knowledge belongs to the man who has no further need to learn because he has finished

learning. No, only that man is really knowing who understands that he must keep learning over and over again, and who above all, on the basis of this understanding, has attained to the point where he is always *able to learn*. This is much more difficult than to possess information.

The importance of recognizing the mild hold man has on understanding shows up in another area where absolutes seem to hold sway. There is written, and indeed it is sometimes carved in stone, "Ye shall know the truth and the truth shall set you free." Impressive and essentially unarguable—provided the word "truth" is not made of stone.

Awareness of the excess of ignorance over knowledge leads to the acceptance of a proposition to the effect that truth changes in the light of greater understanding. One need look only at the effect brought about by Copernicus' nonacceptance of the "truth" of the solar system as he had learned about it.

So ignorance is with us. It is possible to distinguish between that of the individual and that of mankind, but it does not follow that the ignorance of man is the sum of the ignorance of each of us. The current, sometimes-lamented information explosion has had a twofold effect. For one, it can be seen more nearly as an understanding compression. In other words, theories and models of the physical world and the world of man and men become more effective in relating otherwise unrelated facts, observations, and experiences. Secondly, at the same time it has shown us vast additional areas of incomprehension. That is, it has produced a simultaneous ignorance explosion.

The stockpile of the individual ignorance is more or less measurable for each of us. But that of man is itself part of the ignorance. There are no bounds. The ignorance stockpile is high and wide, and it stretches in all directions.

The ignorance of the individual can be markedly diminished by education. This does not necessarily mean education of the formal kind, since in the final analysis all learning must be done by the self. Formal education provides useful facilities, direct help, and stimulation. Systematic education is more likely found in schools, and for this reason, perhaps, the school is often considered the sole educational source, an unsupportable proposition. Each of us ultimately must capture understanding in his own way.

The vast amount of discussion regarding teaching as a means of instilling thoughtfulness in young minds is impressive if only for the fact that it generally does not recognize that those truly understanding of real ignorance are the best preceptors. The know-it-all, one frequently with only superficial acquaintance with the material at hand, generally inspires no more than a parallel superficial interest in understanding. On the other hand, those with genuine understanding of the ignorance which remains associated with true insight have a true and valuable quality in inducing learning. This is so especially for those in regions beyond the current understanding of mankind. Otherwise stated, those ignorant of what we know are best led to understanding by those respectful of what we do not yet know.

There has been much said and written that leads to an unfortunate conclusion which holds that training is somehow denigrating. Yet the most philosophic amongst us, the most artistically creative amongst us, the most articulate and literate amongst us, have perforce been trained. Whether by self, by others, or by some combination is less important than the realization that tooling to increase skills and to apply what we understand to a problem at hand is consistent with sophisticated human endeavor.

Most of us are more apt at problem solving than at "pure" creation. And most with original creative abilities are more or less minor creators. Only a very small percentage supply the great and vital thrusts which shape the major pathways to new levels of insight and perception. Yet neither can do without the other. The outline of a whole great area of ignorance can be shown only by the few great ones, but the full delineation of the area is done by the near great, the good, and the competent. Adaptation to use, whether for the mind and spirit or for the body and its surroundings, is made by those who understand the hazily defined regions of lately discerned relevant ignorance plus the needs and desires of man. Then the rest of us rationalize and integrate this whole into our storehouses of understanding.

Each of us finds different aspects of man's real knowledge incomprehensible. Each of us finds some aspects of man's real knowledge more or less comprehensible. The susceptible material can be got by labor and by intelligence to a degree which varies considerably from person to person. There are, however, certain aspects of man's real knowledge which are more or less incomprehensible to each of us to a degree which again depends on each of us.

This incomprehensible material leads variously to superstition, or to faith, or to a vigorous creative attack. Which one or another of these paths is chosen must necessarily depend on the quality and vitality of the mind as it approaches the problem. It is notable that the path to creativity which constantly produces change always leaves the setting the same; namely, paths toward faith, toward superstition, or toward creativity in any of its forms.

It is worth recognizing that facts and knowledge are not equatable. Knowledge involves understanding of facts, and it follows that when definable ignorance stands before us, the work-bag requires both tools. When we finally develop insight into the missing link, we inevitably translate some of the bare facts at our disposal into knowledge. We do this by working with them and coming to understanding by virtue of this labor, a true bootstrap operation.

The ignorance of mankind itself is divisible into essentially two gross segments much like those described above. There is that which is definable in terms of objectives perceived with rough paths already laid out; there is that which is undefinable and which can be called pure ignorance.

In the first case, the lack in continuity or the missing links are recognizable. Here we are more or less ignorant in a discernible way. This falls into the area of problem solving because insightful people can attack the problem with relevant knowledge and achieve a perceived objective. Here, the important thing is to recognize and isolate the need and then to bring to bear the appropriate fruitful minds with the necessary store of facts and knowledge.

This form of realization of our ignorance, then, provides specific problems requiring solutions, and this leads to ascertainable specific approaches. John Dewey believed that from these "problematic," "conflicting," or "tensional" situations, as he called them, "reflection appears as the dominant trait of a situation when there is something seriously the matter. Given such a situation, it is obvious that the meaning of the situation as a whole is uncertain." This is from the introduction to his *Essays on Experimental Logic.* He further held that the true understanding of theories and the rational explanation of data come only from the tension encountered when there is a contradiction between theory and experiment. From chapter three of his *Studies in Logical Theory,*

> It is *in* this conflict and because of it that the matters or contents, or significant quales, stand out as such. As long as the sun revolves about the earth without tension or question, this single "content" or fact, is not in any way abstracted *as* content or object.

Currently we have brought into focus a large number of societal problems which require pooling our understanding, as well, perhaps, as pooling our ignorance, in order to provide some prospect of solution. Indeed, certain conclusions already are clear; for instance, societal problems have no unique solutions. Thus, the best that can be done is to provide potential solutions and to produce a priority order for those solutions. The application of experience to knowledge in a complex problem area and the constant feedback to see whether the solutions are useful or not, and the reasons for either, provide a further path for the production of potential solutions for these large systemic problems.

The second area is that which is pure, that is, it is not yet even defined. This is the area in which those who have the creative ability as well as the fortitude and energy produce more or less major changes in that which we call truth. It is in this area, whether it be philosophic, artistic, or scientific, that the truth changes in the light of newer understanding. This is a philosophy often hard to accept, since a truth once perceived and understood becomes a part of the arsenal of the mind and is not easily given up. This is one quality of thought which, although generally not detrimental, does sometimes function to inhibit further understanding. Clearly, a delicate balance is needed.

It is important to iterate and reiterate almost to the point of absurdity that creative activity is not restricted to the artist with a palette or a performer at the keyboard, and that research is not restricted to the natural scientist working at a laboratory bench. So when one talks of a new tone pattern or of the production of a new super-heavy chemical element or of a new insight into the effect of full freedom on group behavior, these are not different aspects of human activity. They all fall within the purview of original work done by original minds.

Creative work is a vital societal force. It, like all human activities, contains a certain amount of sham and fraud introduced by those who choose to use it for that purpose. It is best done by those with a basic, innate honesty who can tolerate criticism and still maintain sufficient equilibrium to attempt new ideas and new insights in a dark, vague, and formless whole.

The mission of those who do this kind of original work is the reduction of ignorance. Only no matter where or what kind, it is largely a random approach to our lack of understanding and is difficult to justify accountably. Creative work, whether it be in music, philosophy, art, or the pursuit of mathematics, ordinarily has no direct bearing on those problems which currently face us. Yet in terms of the fulfillment of the mind and the body, the fragments which each such creative worker lays upon the shelf for the future may well be useful, may well, indeed, be necessary for the continued well-being of the race.

It is certainly frustrating that we cannot predict reliably which fragments are needed and when. Before the fact, the most wise and the most experienced among us can judge the suitability of a given program of creative work only on the basis of the current quality of the individual most concerned with it and his thoughts on the quest. On occasion during the course of development of an object, or process, or composition, we recognize a lack of understanding or knowledge, and we can then predetermine what is necessary to fill the gap.

So it can be seen that ignorance surrounds us, and that it is in a stockpile higher than anyone can see and broader than anyone can visualize. It is diminished by experience, and it is diminished in each of us by firm and constant activity. That which is part of the ignorance of all of us can be diminished by a managed program of research and training. Some of it must be diminished by a stochastic process which depends wholly on flights of individual imagination. We see that problems can be solved by thoughtful approaches which can only provide priorities or options, and that the large problems which face us all as a part of the species have few if any yes or no answers.

This whole matter perhaps can best be summed up by a parable noted by Morris Abram (p. 62, *Southern University Conference Report*, 1973). He spoke of the Chinese master Won Lo and the five students who had been with him for many years. Recognizing the approach of his own demise, Won Lo decided it was time to choose one of his students to succeed him as master. He asked each student to take a room and furnish it in the manner he deemed most appropriate to all that he had learned. Won Lo's choice would be based on the way each treated his room. The first student furnished his room tastefully with the most delightful objects of art; the second filled his room with musicians and their instruments. The third and fourth students also furnished their rooms with fine objects they had learned of in their studies. In each case Won Lo commented on the sophistication and high quality of mind of those who could so well perceive the beauties and values of the world.

However, it was to the fifth student that Won Lo handed his mantle. The room of this student was totally bare, and in it he walked forward holding aloft a lighted candle. Won Lo saw that he was the only one of the five who realized that truth must be continually sought after in a world of ignorance and unknowns.

WHITEHEAD'S METAPHYSICAL SYSTEM*

CHARLES HARTSHORNE

As is well known, Alfred North Whitehead (b. 1861) was a teacher of mathematics and theoretical physics in England. With his student Bertrand Russell, he wrote the major work of mathematical logic, *Principia Mathematica*. He made various contributions to mathematics and to the philosophy of science, as well as to the theory of education. From the beginning, he studied philosophy and was interested in it, but without neglecting history and theology. It is evident that he also had considerable interest in biology. The scope of his knowledge and interest reminds one of Leibniz and, before Leibniz, of Plato. These are the three thinkers who sought to unite, so far as possible, mathematics, metaphysics, religion, and scientific cosmology, and who had the knowledge and intellectual powers required to do so. Descartes, C. S. Peirce, and Russell belong to the same type, but hardly on the same level. Whitehead is especially like Plato in that, despite his capacity to think clearly, i.e., mathematically, he never deceived himself into believing that he could think everything with clarity so that

*A translation of Charles Hartshorne, "Das metaphysische System White-heads," *Zeitschrift für philosophische Forschung* 3, no. 4 (1949): 566–75. Translated by Schubert M. Ogden.

whatever he could not so think could be simply eliminated from the world.

Everyone who knew Whitehead personally marveled at him as a human being. I myself have never known anyone who so strongly impressed me by his genius and kindness. Kant made a similar impression on his acquaintances, although he was rather drier and more purely intellectual.

I will now try to characterize Whitehead as a metaphysician and to sketch the outlines of his system.

1. Whitehead is in the highest degree a rationalist. He once defined rationalism as the search for the coherence of the presuppositions of civilized life. But with Socrates he recognizes that these presuppositions cannot be derived with certainty from the ordinary meanings of words. He knows just as well as anyone else that in everyday life we have to speak of persons and physical things, and that we also have need of religious concepts in order to grasp the deeper meaning of life. But he is much freer than Leibniz and Spinoza in recognizing the inexactness and ambiguity and the all but unavoidable error that attaches to traditional thoughts about these things if one takes them as absolute or literal truths. In daily life, Whitehead thinks, such general concepts are only as exact and unambiguous as everyday purposes require; but the grasp of the general elements of life and of being purely in themselves, such as philosophy strives for, is deeply opposed to these everyday purposes. The latter always have to do with what is more or less special, and to this end one *uses* general concepts without grasping them altogether clearly. The circumstances of such use, of the living context, give the concepts a sufficiently unambiguous meaning. But philosophy seeks to abstract from all such special circumstances in order to see and to describe the generalities themselves as clearly and unambiguously as possible. This, according to Whitehead, is almost infinitely difficult, and the learned tradition has made it much too easy, remaining naive and unreliable in spite of its appearance of tireless exactitude. Such concepts as "substance," "soul," "thing," undoubtedly have a meaning that can well be taken up into a

coherent system. But this is possible only if one remains conscious of the harmless and yet immense simplification and abridgment that take place in the ordinary use of these concepts and brings this to expression in his philosophical explanations.

There is another sense in which Whitehead is a rationalist. In this sense, which is perhaps closer to the historical meaning of the word, rationalism is the search for the necessary truths, the truths whose contradictories are unthinkable. But the earlier rationalists propounded doctrines whose contradictories can very well be thought. They simply made no effort to think them. For example, they asserted that *all* truths are eternal, even though the concept of newly emergent truths, which are insofar *not* eternal, contains no contradiction and is by no means unthinkable. A proposition is true that corresponds to some reality; hence, so long as there still is no such reality, no proposition can correspond to it. Thus, if new realities emerge, new truths also emerge. Unless everything whatsoever is eternal, not all truth can be eternal. Another example: Leibniz and the other classical rationalists assumed that the subject of a true proposition is ultimately something identical through time—like a soul, say, rather than a once-for-all occurrence or event, like a momentary experience. And yet it is thinkable that the basic form of truth describes precisely events or experiences, not souls or other so-called substances. Whitehead, along with others, shows that the doctrine of substance leads to contradictions that can be avoided by a doctrine of events. He also shows that the values intended by the concept "soul" or "person," or even of "physical thing," do not need to be lost in such a doctrine. Still another example: Spinoza, Leibniz, and other rationalists assumed that we must think of God as a being that is in every respect immutable, entirely necessary, never passive or contingent. Whitehead, however, establishes the possibility, perhaps even the necessity, of a concept of God as, on the one hand, in his "primordial nature," eternally immutable and unconditionally necessary, while, on the other hand, in his "consequent nature," ever newly emerging and containing accidents. In other words, God exists necessarily and has necessary attributes, but these are not his sole attributes; he also has contingent attributes, which are not eternal, although they are indestructible and immortal.

2. Whitehead is also an empiricist, and that, too, in the highest degree. But the so-called empiricists of the past have forgotten or denied precisely the deepest experiences, the most general things that are empirically given. What is experience if one abstracts, for instance, from recollection or from memory? Of course, Locke and Hume were well aware that we only *know* of experience through recollection. But they did not recognize that experience itself, in its very essence, has the structure of recollection, that the temporality of experience, for example, depends on this. Or, again, the empiricists assumed that feelings and passions are sheer additions to the knowing functions of perceiving and thinking. In truth, however, as Whitehead seeks to show, life essentially is a matter of valuing, purposing, suffering, and enjoying, from which mere knowing and mere perceiving are only abstractions and derived phenomena. The empiricists supposed that we directly and immediately experience mere ideas or subjective feelings, which then serve us as signs for physical objects. Whitehead helps us to see that one immediately experiences certain processes in one's own body, which can then indeed be regarded, and ordinarily are regarded, as signs for things outside of the body. Thus the basic experience on which perceiving rests is the immediate givenness neither of ideas nor of the things we see with our eyes and touch with our hands, but rather of the eyes and hands themselves, along with other parts of the body, especially parts of the brain or nervous system. These inner bodily occurrences or processes are not consciously grasped as such, for our consciousness has the tendency to experience and use what goes on in the body merely as a symbol for the external world—somewhat as when reading a book one does not think of the letters on the pages but of the things with which the book has to do. Add to this that the internal processes are not clearly experienced in their details—and only a divine experience can clearly grasp the detailed contents of its objects. In general, the

clarity of human experience of the body extends only so far as is necessary to provide usable signs of the external world. The signs are experienced, the outer world being thereby shown or presented somewhat as on a map. And yet the signs are not mere ideas or one's own feelings, but, rather, real parts of the subhuman physical world, which consists of cells, molecules, etc. Even so, the signs are affective, essentially of the nature of experience. They have nothing whatever to do with mere dead matter. Nerves are living organisms, and, according to Whitehead, they have their own world of feelings. To this point we shall presently return.

3. Whitehead is rightly called a realist. As we have just seen, what is immediately experienced in perception on his view are bodily processes, not mere ideas or one's own feelings. But in order to grasp and assess the radicality of his realism we must recur to the theme of recollection. For Whitehead, as for Bergson, the basic level of recollection, or, better, of memory, is not merely a present state that *refers to* the past and permits an *inference* about it, but, rather, an immediate experience, a direct grasp and intuition of a past event. To be past does not mean to have passed out of existence altogether, but to be something that ever continues to exist in relation to memory or as the object of memory. The present experience relates itself to past experiences and is dependent on them. Thus the present experience as subject depends on the past as its object. This establishes one side of realism, which affirms that knowing depends on the known. The other side of realism affirms that the known, "the object," is independent of the given subject. The past experience, which is an object of memory, has no internal relation to this state of remembering. My recollection is not that my previous experience referred to or anticipated precisely this momentary state of recollection. An experience is always ignorant of the manner in which it will subsequently be remembered. To be sure, there are anticipations. But they have to do only with rather vague, for the most part very general and abstract attributes of the future, not with concrete, individual future experiences. Consequently, we never experience tem-

poral relations between concrete individuals prospectively but always only retrospectively. Succeeding is a real self-relation, which consists in memory; but preceding is not a real self-relation, and being *prior to* is not a real relation between individuals, for one never finds a future experience given in its concreteness in the experience of the present moment. Anticipating not only has a reverse temporal direction from recalling; it also has an essentially different character: it is a relation not to the concrete but rather to the more or less abstract. We anticipate the next day as a date on the calendar, as a political situation, as a certain state of weather, etc. But the past we still have in feeling as a series of individual details or events. As Whitehead says, to observe this, one best takes not such long stretches of time as an entire day, but, rather, quite short stretches of, say, half a second. What is thus experienced is always still there as a concrete experience. In this way, memory provides the example of a realistic relation to an object independent of the subject. The experience, or the subject now remembering, relates itself to the remembered object, while the object does not thus relate itself to the remembering subject, and so is independent of it. This is the principle of realism.

4. Yet it is precisely Whitehead's realism that makes him an idealist in a clearly definable sense of the word. The object of a remembering experience is in itself also an experience and hence is likewise a subject. One remembers the fact that he had already remembered; he recalls his recollections. In this case, the object is also a subject. But it is not the same subject, for the remembered subject does not have just *this* recollection but, as was said before, is ignorant in relation to it. Hence two subjects must be present: one which knows, and one which does not know, with respect to one and the same relation of recalling. A concrete individual is here a subject and has another concrete individual as its object. But the latter also is a subject that has its own objects, and so on. By this example, we see that the realistic independence of the known from this particular act of knowing is quite compatible with the possibility that the object can also be a subject. Indeed, we can go even further: Whitehead believes

that, in the case of *all* the examples possible of realism, the clearer their realistic character stands out, the clearer their confirmation of idealism. In addition to the case of memory, where one reexperiences his own earlier experiences as objects, there is the other particularly clear case of one's experiences of his own body. Take, for instance, toothache. Pain is something subjective, psychic. But it is not a mere idea or a feeling that belongs solely to me. I do not pain myself when I suffer a toothache. Something is inflicted on me that pains me, something that is not identical with myself; and I must become conscious of this something through some quality of its own. Yet what pains me has no quality as given unless it is that of the existing pain itself. (I assume, for the sake of simplicity, that in the moment of pain I neither touch the tooth with my finger or tongue nor see it in a mirror.) There is no quality of the thing that pains me given in my experience other than the quality of the pain. Nevertheless, something-not-identical-with-me is present, and this must have some kind of quality. The solution of the paradox lies in the assumption that there is something in addition to my self that also suffers pain. This suffering something can be conceived as a group of bodily cells. Once again, we see that the object itself has subjective character; for whatever can suffer pain must be a subject in the broadest sense of the word. Whitehead thinks that precisely in the cases of pain and—as one can add—of bodily pleasure, we undoubtedly have to do with a not-self. And just this is our basic relation to our body. What we learn of the body through seeing and touching is an addition, a mere further development of our original bodily relationship, which is one of suffering and enjoying.

Thus the world is given to us primarily and most certainly as the body, and this as essentially affective, not as mere matter. The given qualities of the physical world as immediately given are subjective qualities. But how about the qualities of the external senses? Are they, too, subjective and affective? Yes, Whitehead holds, and as a fact that can be experienced and observed. It is the open secret of aesthetic experiences and of art that sense qualities have an affective, "emotional" character, that they have the values of feeling. Whitehead claims that the learned tradition in philosophy has inverted the truth about this, for it assumes that affective qualities are mere additions to sense qualities. The truth, however, is that it is specific feelings, passions, and values that are original, a pure, value-free quality being only a limiting case or a fiction of abstract thought. It is not true that feelings are added to sense qualities through external association, but, to the contrary, the fiction of the pure sense quality has arisen only through intellectual association. This line of thought is not new, and one finds it in certain recent German philosophers, e.g., Rickert, also Heidegger, and earlier in Bishop Berkeley.

5. Whitehead, so far as I can tell, is the first to develop a clear, systematic ontology of relations, an ontological doctrine of relations. Real relations, according to him, exist only if something in itself is related to something else. A real relation between A and B must either be a property of at least one of them or else constitute a third reality, which must in turn be related—again giving rise to the same problem unless something is present that has an internal relation to some other thing. Relations presuppose that something relates itself to something else. This says two things. First, relations exist only when something is really relative. In the case of the pure absolute, or the nonrelative, there is no relation. Indeed, the nonrelative, or absolute, presupposes the relative, as every no presupposes a yes. Thus, to understand relations, we must conceive the relative or that which is dependent on others. Second, if anything new comes to be, if anything new is made, relations also must come to be and be made anew. Hence the coming to be of a relation is an act, a creation. And this act has to belong to the same relative something that has the relation itself; for, if one presupposes otherwise, one must still assume a relation between whatever performs the act and whatever has the new relation, and so one again confronts the same problem of the coming to be of a new relation. An explanation of relations is possible only on the basis of there being something relative, which relates itself to others. If nothing can relate itself, then

nothing can be related to anything else. Consequently, we face the question, What is it that relates itself to another? Or, what is it whose relativity is its own act?

The answer is given in the realistic doctrine that the subject, or an actual knowing, depends on its object, on that which is known. For knowing is an act, and, since dependence and relativity are the same, knowing is an act that creates relations in itself. Knowing is not anything that simply happens to one; it is something that one does, and in this doing there is an internal relatedness to the object, to that which is known. In order to express this, Whitehead chooses the word "prehend." The basic element of relatedness is not *apprehension*, for that is a special case, where certain higher functions of comparison or consciousness are involved, but, rather, *prehension*. An experience as an experience of something is active, self-constituting, relative. Not that what is experienced, the object, is thereby constituted; for, according to Whitehead's realism, the object is independent of this, as of every other particular experience. The relation to the object, however, is brought into being by the experience. Knowing in its most general and primitive form, as pure having or grasping, *prehension*, is precisely not relationless, as Rehmke asserted, but the primal form of all real relations. Thence arises an argument for idealism as the doctrine that all reality consists in subjects or experiences. It is the subject, as we have seen, that is the home of relations and, indeed, as acts, as becoming and not as mere being. But the real object must also belong to the world of occurrences. Only if such a real object is itself also a subject, a second subject or experience, does it, too, have its relations as its acts, as its prehensions. If I think about my earlier recollections, for example, I thereby relate myself to things that were themselves previously self-related. In this way, the sequence extends indefinitely. The world is constructed out of such sequences of relations. Time is precisely the sequence of self-relating events. If these events are subjects or experiences, we know wherein this temporal relatedness consists. If they are not subjects, we must seek the relativity of time somewhere else than in the subject-object relation.

Naturally, we can simply say that relation in time is pure succession. But the question is how this relation is actually experienced. For, if it is experienced nowhere, we can know nothing about it, and the word "succession" is meaningless. We say for instance, "The leaves are on the ground 'after' they were on the tree." But where is this "after"? What *has* this relation and is *experienced* as having it? Does one *see* from the fallen leaf that it is now fallen and once was on the tree? One *knows* this about the leaf but one does not *see* it as a quality of the leaf. Nothing about the leaf as now seen is such a relation to the tree. Our memory tells us that the cause of the leaf's lying on the ground is its having been on the tree. Still, as Hume shows, one sees this relation neither on the tree nor on the leaf. But if *I* have climbed the tree and am now standing on the ground again, I do indeed intuit the having been on the tree in myself as a quality of my present existence, or at least as a past experience of the same kind. That is the basic phenomenon of memory. What we should have learned from Hume is that we can find a clear case of relatedness or relativity only in the subject. If one skeptically rejects this case, then one can know in no intelligible way that there is any such thing as a succession of experiences.

From this we see that it is the *relativity* of the subject, not what certain idealistic schools assumed to be its absoluteness, which is the basis of true idealism. And this very relativity is a basic thesis also of realism. Thus the conflict between idealism and realism ends in an alliance that not only is free of contradiction but is even demanded by both sides. If memory, in howsoever primitive a form, is present even in atoms, molecules, and all genuine individuals as such, then, and only then, "succession" as a relation has an experienceable and intelligible meaning. This is the idealistic factor, whereas the independence of the remembered from this act of remembering furnishes the realistic factor.

Causality is the other side of the same problem. If the future will have memory, then I already know something about it. The future must be an experience that at least would be able to look back on our present. But not every kind of experience is compatible with the recollection of a certain kind of past experience. I cannot enjoy the consciousness of having done only good yesterday if I have to look back on what I did as in some respects bad. There are laws governing the compatibility of elements in experience. That an experience is *one* experience, however, means that there is a certain accommodation or adaptation of its factors to one another. This accommodation is aesthetic in the sense that its laws are best known to the artist. Of course, an experience is possible even of the ugly. But the ugly is never absolute and is always a kind of broken harmony, as a number of aestheticians have pointed out. If no aesthetic accommodation is attainable, there simply is no experience. For example, if one loses consciousness from a blow on the head, this is because the processes in the brain no longer offer a sufficiently harmonious object for our immediate experience of the body. In that moment, the aesthetic problem becomes insoluble for us.

Yet one further step, and the problem of causality is in principle solved. Either there is a possibility that all aesthetic problems might become insoluble, so that all experience would vanish into nothing, or else there is something that precludes this catastrophe and is always concerned that in every case some solution be possible. This is the deepest basis of order in the world and, according to Whitehead, is a function of God. Order is the possibility of aesthetic accommodation and is attained by the fact that all experiences are so guided or influenced that they can present the future with none but soluble problems. That one is forced to lose consciousness means only that in cases of this kind aesthetic accommodation at the level of human experience is excluded, even though on another level it is not excluded. The world process continues. That it will always continue is the power of God, who sets certain limits to disharmony. Which leads us, finally, to the theme of Whitehead's concept of the divine.

6. Whitehead is a theist, although not in the traditional sense, according to which theism and pantheism are sheer opposites. He has found a higher synthesis which is about equally far from

classical theism and from classical pantheism. According to theism, God is entirely independent of the world, not only in his existence, but in all his attributes. He is the pure absolute, the utterly unrelative. For pantheism, on the other hand, God has no independence from the world at all; he is the unity of the world, none of whose parts could have been otherwise. Common to the two doctrines, however, is the dubious supposition that God in his essence is simple, in such fashion that if attributes like absolute or eternal belong to him, it is impossible for such opposite attributes as relative and temporal also to belong to him. But why cannot God be in one respect absolute and eternal, while in another respect relative and temporal? Attributes such as p and not-p contradict one another only if they are supposed to belong to one and the same subject in the same respect. A man, for instance, can remain unchanged in the goodness of his actions, even though his sense experiences change, and even though his actions themselves change. Changed and unchanged, therefore, are compatible in a concrete subject, provided only that this subject is not utterly simple and of a single nature. According to Whitehead, as according to Bergson, the unchangeable, that which does not become in time, the eternal, is something abstract in reality, not its entire content. Mere being is an element of becoming, not becoming an element of being. To attain to pure being from the becoming of experience, we have to abstract from all temporal changes. We cannot proceed conversely from mere being and from it abstract becoming. This is the real meaning of Aristotle's great doctrine of the eternal forms, namely, that they exist solely in the concrete process of becoming and cannot exist separated from it in and for themselves. The unchangeable form is something abstract, general, which is included in the concrete-particular. Applied to God (Aristotle, unfortunately, overlooked this application), this doctrine means that, if God has an unchangeable form, this is not his concrete individual reality but something abstract in it. The concrete God would be a becoming, and the eternal form, an abstract attribute which is common to every phase of this becoming. Whitehead calls this abstract form of

God his "primordial nature," while the concrete divine reality constitutes "the consequent nature of God."

If we reflect on the religious meaning of the concept of God, we discover that Whitehead's doctrine makes possible an unforced acknowledgment of certain religious values. God as the object of love and devotion is thought of as a person, who is himself capable of loving. But love is a self-relating, a relativity toward the beloved. Traditional theism, which conceives God solely as absolute, could not speak of God's love for his creatures without inconsistency. Yet, since, according to Whitehead, God has a consequent nature which is eminently relative, being even the most extreme case of relativity, there is no inconsistency in asserting that God loves us. Only the eternal abstract form in God is absolute, dependent on nothing, influenced by nothing, and unchanged.

But is this God with a dipolar nature a personal God? Whitehead does not directly raise or answer this question, although he does so indirectly. What is a person? Concretely considered, it is a stream of experiences and acts, a sequence of events, in which an individual character, a complex of personal qualities, again and again expresses itself in various ways. The character is not the concrete human being, not its acts and experiences, but, rather, the *tendency* to give all of these a unique individual style. Character is not reality, but the law for countless possible realities, for it is the style or tendency toward a specific *way* of acting and experiencing. The latter clearly are what is real or concrete in a man, while the way, the style, or the tendency is something relatively abstract, virtual. When a man dies, there remains much that is otherwise possible which is left undone, unactualized. A man with good character will, given suitable circumstances, perform many good deeds. If he has to do with a beggar, he will do the right thing; if he has to do with a rich friend, he will act in another way, and yet not less well, not less in the style of his character. In short, character is something relatively unchangeable, but also abstract, in the stream of concrete becoming.

Returning to the problem of God, we note that, for

Whitehead, God cannot die. His character is eternal, and he can never acquire any other character. His goodness is "primordial," a primal factor in all becoming, and also immortal. Nor does it ever change. But, as we have seen, goodness is nothing concrete. Concrete life is not merely ethical, but also aesthetic in its value. Goodness is only a certain stylistic tendency according to which the concrete occurs. God always acts and experiences in his style of perfect goodness and wisdom. The style as such is always and absolutely the same. But it by no means follows that the actions or experiences of God are *in every respect* the same and unchangeable. The primordial nature is the stylistic tendency of the divine experiencing. The consequent nature is his experiencing itself, whose content is the world. This is the religious notion of a truly personal, living, and loving God. A similar notion of God can be found in the later writings of Schelling and in Fechner's *Zend Avesta*, although in these cases not as part of a system as grand and as clearly developed as Whitehead's. Some theologians of our time, including Berdyaev, Niebuhr and several others, also appear to have such an idea of God, though for the most part less definitely and unambiguously.

But is God, so conceived, to be considered the Creator? One can say so, on the assumption that one understands creation as religion understands it, i.e., if the religious insight into the fundamental role of love in the universe is upheld. In the relation of love, individuals receive their reality to a certain extent from one another. My friend, for example, gives me that part of my reality which he himself presents in my experience as the object of my love. Now our love of God is our most fundamental relation of love, and God as the object of our love is our one essential object, the one who is always there, in whose consequent nature all the beauty of the world is contained. God gives us himself as the object of our experience; the grasp, or *prehension,* of this object, however, must be our own act. In this sense, the creature to a certain extent creates itself. Whitehead speaks boldly of "the self-created creature." But this self-creation is possible only on the basis of the proffered beauty of

God. As Aristotle said, without explaining what this could mean in his system, God guides the world as a beloved his lover. God inspires us in the depths of our feelings. Whether religiously minded or not, we all live from an unconscious affective grasp of ideals and purposes that are present in the consciousness of God. As Augustine and Malebranche put it, we see the truth in God. But for Whitehead this has a double meaning: God does indeed inspire us with the vision of his *eternal* purposes, those which are already given in his character, in his primordial nature; but he also inspires us with the vision of the purposes in his consequent nature, which emerge in time and in which the world as it has become is taken into account and evaluated. God constantly guides the world process not only by eternal values and truths but also by the new needs that are always emerging in time. For, as we have seen, there are ever new realities, and so ever new truths about these realities. The eternal principles of value, the basic needs, are these—that monotonous repetition and exaggerated conformity be avoided, but also that novelty and variety not be carried too far. The two great evils are boredom, caused by a lack of contrast, and painful conflict, which means the lack of similarity and unity, whereby experience threatens to be undone by intolerable oppositions and confusion.

But the guidance of the world by the divine purposes does not result in everything's being harmonious and perfect. Since all experience creates itself, or in part emerges spontaneously, God cannot see to it that boredom or painful conflicts never occur. In guiding the world, he can only balance the danger of boredom against that of pain and choose the best possibilities accordingly. He does not choose directly between specific forms but, rather, between their possibilities or probabilities. The creatures themselves choose between the specific forms. Thus God guides the world not in that he makes our decisions for us or eternally determines them, but only in that he so shapes his thoughts and feelings that, when we grasp (prehend) them, we are so attracted by their beauty that we react in an *approximately* determined way. We do what we wish, but what we wish depends on, although it is not fully determined by, how God shapes himself as the object of our subconscious feelings. God can only lure us, he cannot coerce or completely determine us; for experience is something that precisely cannot be coerced or determined. Hence God can shape the creatures in accordance with his will only up to a certain point. Not because his power is any less than maximal, but simply because power over experience can only consist in limiting the possible responses to a given stimulus by this very stimulus itself. Thus what is determined are not the responses but only their range of possibilities. Within this range, the response remains free and uncontrolled, and from this absence of divine control there arise the more or less tragic conflicts in the world. The spontaneity of all experiencing and becoming is responsible for these conflicts, not the will of God. Since everything real consists in spontaneous experiencing, it is meaningless to say, "If God decides to create free creatures, he has to assume responsibility for the way they use their freedom." That there should be free creatures at all is no decision of God's, but lies in the very nature of being and becoming and is inseparable from God's primordial nature. The only thing to be decided is the direction of the development of the creatures' range of freedom. "God is the poet of the world," that is, he guides the world partly by eternal, and partly by ever new, ideals of beauty and harmony.

NOTE

This essay was originally written, and published, in German (*Zeitschrift für Philosophische Forschung*, 1949, III/4, pp. 566–575). The excellent translation into English I owe to Schubert Ogden. For many improvements in the German I am indebted to the late bilingual Olga Pauck (Mrs. Wilhelm Pauck). Thus, to make up for this being an old essay, three people rather than one contribute to this testimony to my cherished friend Rabbi Olan.

Another remark seems necessary. In sections 2 and 3, I ought to have made explicit the very important point that for Whitehead perception and memory have the same temporal structure. In both, the direct data are past, not simultaneous or contemporary, events or experiences. Always what is *prehended* (see section 5, 2nd paragraph) is temporally prior to the prehending experience. We perceive the past as truly as we remember it. For astronomers this is obvious; Whitehead generalizes it for all perception. As I have come to say, since writing this article, perception is impersonal memory; in what is ordinarily called memory it is past experiences of one's own that are given, in perception it is the past of the rest of the world, most directly and vividly the past of one's own bodily processes. In memory we perceive, so to speak, our personal past; in perception we remember, so to speak, the impersonal past, the past of our environment, taking the body, as Whitehead and I do, as that part of environing reality with which we, as minds or souls, most directly interact. In both cases we prehend what has already happened.

PROLEGOMENA TO A CHRISTIAN THEOLOGY OF NATURE

SCHUBERT M. OGDEN

From a Christian standpoint, presumably, man's exploitation of his natural environment originally roots in human sinfulness. In Thomas Beddoe's words,

> Nature's polluted,
> There's man in every secret corner of her
> Doing damned wicked deeds.
> Thou art, old world,
> A hoary, atheistic, murdering star.

But, in recent years, the charge has been made, and with reasons, that modern Western man's exploitative attitude toward nature has its roots, on the contrary, precisely in the Judaeo-Christian, and, specifically, Christian theological tradition itself. According to those who make this charge, the sharp separation Christianity especially has traditionally made between man and nature, on the one hand, and God and nature, on the other, along with its understanding of God's mandate to man to dominate the rest of creation, are the fundamental presuppositions behind the modern development of science and technology and their use to exploit the natural environment for the sake of human ends. It follows, then, that not the least change called for if we are to develop a nonexploitative attitude toward nature, which is a necessary condition of coming to terms with the so-called ecological problem, is the criticism of these traditional theological presuppositions and their replacement by others. Some voices, indeed, have proposed a new kind of religion altogether, a specifically non-Christian kind of religiousness, as essential to any enduring solution to the problem of ecology.

It is also true that others, with even more convincing reason, have challenged this historical analysis of the roots of our ecological crisis and, by implication, the proposals made in order to meet it. Granted that much in the Christian theological tradition has had the effect it is alleged to have had, there have also been countertendencies, and it is a fair question whether they do not have as clear a claim to be biblically founded as the presuppositions singled out for criticism. Also important is the finding of other cultural historians that exploitation of the natural environment, to the point of ecological crisis, has taken place prior to and quite independently of the cultural tradition determined by Judaism and Christianity.

Still, even with this counterargument, whose force seems to me considerable, the question remains whether the Christian tradition, by and large, is not essentially anthropocentric in a way that contributes importantly to how we understand ourselves in relation to nature. Furthermore, it is arguable that modern Christianity, since, roughly, the Renaissance and the Reformation, has become ever more man-centered in its understanding of the natural order. Concurrently with the expansion of the horizon of our understanding of nature, effected by modern science ever since Copernicus and Galileo, there has taken place that "turn to the subject," whose philosophical pioneers were, respectively, Descartes and Kant. It has been in the cultural context determined by this "subjective turn" that modern Christian theology, also, has taken shape—to the point where nothing has become more characteristic of modern Protestant theology, and now, increasingly, Roman Catholic theology as well, than the sharp distinction between history and nature, the sphere of the distinctively human and the rest of the created order.

One illustration of the shift I have in mind is the emergence into almost exclusive dominance of the notion of personal, subjective immortality in modern Christian accounts of man's ultimate destiny. Of course, the idea of subjective immortality as such was incorporated into Christian tradition at a very early date—no later, certainly, than the second century, when the Christian understanding of existence came to be explicated and defended in characteristically Greek religious, cultural, and philosophical terms. But, significantly, it is not of immortality that the ancient creeds of the church speak, but, rather, of resurrection of the dead—or, in the Apostles' Creed, literally, resurrection of the flesh. This idea of resurrection derives from late Jewish apocalypticism, with its projection of hope for the future along a horizontal, rather than, as with the idea of immortality, a vertical line. Although this idea, too, was and remained man-centered, the fact is that the picture it projects of man's ultimate destiny is the picture of "a new heaven and a new earth" (Rev. 21:1; cf. Isa. 65:17), which allows for the participation of all creation in the final fulfillment. So Paul, speaking in the terms of this picture, says that "the creation waits with eager longing for the revealing of the sons of God; for the creation was subjected to futility, not of its own will but by the will of him who subjected it in hope; because the creation itself will be set free from its bondage to decay and obtain the glorious liberty of the children of God. We know that the whole creation has been groaning in travail together until now . . ." (Rom. 8:19 ff.). In modern Christianity, however, this apocalyptic hope for the resurrection of the dead, and hence for the fulfillment in some way of the whole creation in a new heaven and a new earth, has either simply dropped out altogether, or else been secularized, or, at most, become a mere metaphor for man's immortality.

So the question is genuine whether the Christian theological understanding of nature, especially in its modern form, is not such as to encourage, to aid and abet, the exploitative attitude which now threatens us with ecological crisis. Indeed, this question, if pressed, clearly seems to require an affirmative answer. But this, then, leads us to ask whether the primary source of Christian theology, namely, Holy Scripture, itself entails or requires the traditional and modern theological understandings of nature.

I do not propose to give an adequately reasoned answer to this essentially exegetical question. The biblical understanding of nature, or, better, the various understandings of nature documented in the biblical writings, is a complex historical problem, to which, in the nature of the case, no simple solution can be given. Yet I do wish to express my opinion that the Bible generally is by no means as unambiguously man-centered as one might suppose, judging from traditional Christian theology, and, especially, from its modern restatements. Although the Bible clearly assigns man a unique place and role in relation both to the rest of earth's creatures and to God, it is another question whether it endorses the mutual exclusion of man and nature, or of history and nature, which has increasingly marked the main theological tradition since its restatement in the terms of the Greek cultural, religious, and philosophical tradition. Indeed, I think John Cobb makes an exegetically sound point when he says that "there is as much ground for inclusionism as for exclusionism in the Bible. The fateful story of creation represents man as created like the rest, from the dust of the earth. He is co-creature with fish and birds and beasts. The fundamental duality lies between creator and creature, not between man and other animals."[1] I also think with Cobb that "Christian theology has focused more upon the image of God in man than upon man's co-creaturehood with other animals. It has given to the idea of the divine image in man a prominence far greater than it is accorded in the Old Testament." And I also accept the conclusion he draws from this with respect to the task of a contemporary Christian theology of nature: "It is the image of co-creaturehood which we need now to recover without the loss of the biblical sense of man as the apex of creation."[2]

But, as I say, I do not intend to enter into the exegetical arguments that would be necessary to establish the soundness of this opinion as to what the primary source of Christian theology, and thus of a Christian theology of nature, allows or even requires one to say. Part of the reason for this is my conviction that the Bible can be fittingly employed as the primary source and norm for a Christian understanding of existence only by recognizing that what finally counts as genuinely scriptural is not only what is *said* in the Bible or even what is *meant* there—although they, of course, are no more identical in the Bible than in any other written text!—but also what is necessarily *implied* by what the Bible means.

Let me give you an example of what I have in mind that bears directly on our question. Without doubt, the Bible not only says but means that God, and God alone, is the creator of all things, in the sense of being the ultimate source or ground of whatever is or is so much as even possible. But this implies, as the classical theological tradition rightly recognized, that God for the Bible is not simply *a* being but *the* being, and thus, in some sense, is "being itself," or the very principle of reality as such. It evidently follows from this, however, that anything that is or could be at all could not be wholly unlike God. For to be wholly unlike God is to be wholly unlike being itself, and to be wholly unlike being itself is to be quite simply nothing, everything that is anything at all being more than mere nothing, and insofar forth like God himself. In short, given the understanding of both God and the world that the biblical witness necessarily implies, the conclusion follows ineluctably that not only man, but anything whatsoever, must be, in some sense, created in the likeness of God. Whatever the *special* sense, then, in which man may be said to be created *imago Dei*, it cannot exclude that this may also be said in some sense of every creature. This is an example of what I take to be essential to a correct use of Scripture as the source and norm of theology. Without something like this, the Bible becomes little more than a series of prooftexts, with which one can establish virtually anything he pleases. I have considerable confidence, however, that in this case the conclusion that follows from the most fundamental and necessary implications of the scriptural witness is also expressly confirmed by most of what Scripture in fact says and means on this issue.

For our purposes here, however, I ask that you simply assume with me that Scripture warrants an understanding of man and nature according to which man is not excluded from nature but included within it, albeit as a co-creature who has a unique place and role in the natural order. The question arising then, given this assumption, is how this scriptural understanding is to be explicated and defended—such explication and defense being essential tasks of a Christian theology of nature. Theology, as the fully reflective understanding of the Christian witness of faith as decisive for human existence, perforce requires concepts wherewith to achieve the understanding that it is its task to achieve. Ultimately, these concepts will be *philosophical* concepts of some kind; for only concepts having the generality and precision of properly philosophical concepts are fit for such a purpose. But, more than that, the Christian understanding of nature can be vindicated as meaningful and true only by showing that it is in fact warranted by a philosophical under-standing of the natural order. For, however appropriately Christian, because scriptural, such an understanding may be, its understandability to human existence, which is to say, its meaning and truth, still remains to be determined. And such determination necessarily entails the employment of *some* philosophical concepts, since such concepts alone are able to do the job of determining its meaning and truth. The question to which we are finally led, then, is what Rudolf Bultmann speaks of as the question of "the 'right' philosophy," by which I mean that philosophical conceptualization of man and nature which, in addition to being meaningful and true on the basis of our shared experience and reflection, provides us with the concepts necessary for explicating and vindicating the understanding of man and nature warranted by the witness of faith attested in Holy Scripture.

To give an adequate answer to this question of the "right" philosophy would require one to do vastly more than I have any intention of attempting here. I simply want to record my conviction that process philosophy, at least of a certain type, must be reckoned as one of the leading contenders for the distinction of being the "right" philosophy in this sense of the words. Actually, having recorded this conviction, I also want to say enough by way of explaining its meaning to indicate some of the reasons I share it.

I would remind you, first of all, that process philosophy of all types presupposes the emergence in the nineteenth century, and, critically, with the Darwinian theory of the evolution of biological species, of an evolutionary scientific world-picture. I say all the process philosophies presuppose such a scientific world-picture because, in one way or another, all of them are efforts to generalize this kind of a world-picture to the point where its principles approach or become universal explanatory principles, which is to say, *philosophical* principles. Also typical of the process philosophies is a reversal of what was not uncommonly taken to be the implication of biological evolution for the understanding of man and his relation to nature. For many persons, in the nineteenth century especially, the clear implication of man's having descended from earlier, nonhuman forms of life was the reduction of man to nothing more than an animal. Given the widely prevalent assumptions as to what nonhuman nature generally, as well as animal nature in particular, amounted to—namely, in Cartesian terms, more or less complex machines utterly lacking in inwardness—this reduction of man to the status of an animal was the denial that even man had any inwardness, much less the spirit, or the unique inwardness, that had traditionally been claimed for him by theology as well as philosophy. But, as the process philosophers typically recognized, the thoroughgoing animality of man was only one of the implications that could be drawn from the evolutionary thesis that human life is, in fact, continuous with life generally. On the face of it, the inference was also permitted that, just because man has emerged from nature, nature itself must be conceived differently from the dominant conception of modern Western science and philosophy. In other words, there was as much reason to interpret nature by analogy with man as to interpret man after the analogy with nature.

Following up this important reversal of thought, the process philosophies all developed understandings of nature in which all living things, certainly, if not all inorganic things as well, have an inward as well as an outward aspect—are in some sense values for themselves and for one another, as well as for that uniquely understanding and evaluating other who is man. The most thoroughgoing and consistent formulation of this insight is represented by Whitehead's metaphysics, which, asserting "the reformed subjectivist principle," develops the claim that "the whole universe consists of elements disclosed in the analysis of the experiences of subjects"—or, as Whitehead also puts it, that "all final individual actualities have the metaphysical character of occasions of experience."[3] And so, in place of the Cartesian-Newtonian picture of nonhuman nature as "dead," Whitehead projects the picture of "nature alive," going so far as to argue that "the energetic activity considered in physics is the emotional intensity entertained in life."[4] According to this revised philosophical picture, then, the *absolute* distinctions between man and nature, or history and nature, all become merely *relative* distinctions. Since even nonhuman nature is not mere matter in motion, but an incredibly complex hierarchy of levels of experience—from the least physical particle all the way up to distinctively human reflectiveness—even nonhuman nature is, in its way, or at its various levels, historical. Indeed, reality as such, or in principle, is interpreted in *historical* terms, it being the metaphysical nature of things that, as Whitehead puts it in defining his basic concept "creativity," "the many become one and are increased by one."[5]

Now it is this typically Whiteheadian understanding of the very nature of reality, and thus of nonhuman nature as well as of man, as genuinely historical in character, which seems to me to provide the sort of philosophical conceptualization that an adequate Christian theology of nature requires. The split between man and the rest of nature is closed by not only naturalizing man but also historicizing the rest of nature. And this understanding is all the more to be taken seriously, because, for all of his stress on the thoroughgoing continuity of man with nature, Whitehead makes clear both that and why man nevertheless has a unique relation not only to the rest of creation but also to its ultimate ground and end, which is to say, God. "The life of a human being," he says, "receives its worth, its importance, from the way in which unrealized ideals shape its purposes and tinge its actions. The distinction between men and animals is in one sense only a difference in degree. But the extent of the degree makes all the difference. The Rubicon has been crossed."[6] And what marks this crossing? Whitehead's answer is clear: "The animals enjoy structure. They can build nests and dams: they can follow the trail of scent through the forest. The concrete realized facts, confused and intermixed, dominate animal life. Man understands structure. He abstracts its dominating principle from the welter of detail. He can imagine alternative illustration. He constructs distant objectives. He can compare the variety of issues. He can aim at the best. But the essence of this human control of purposes depends on the understanding of structure in its variety of applications. To be human requires the study of structure. To be animal merely requires its enjoyment."[7]

Thus what makes man uniquely different from the animal life out of which he has emerged is *understanding*—or, as Whitehead can also say, in more objective or behavioristic terms, *language or speech*. "Language, as commonly understood in the most simple-minded way, stands out as the habitual effect of thought, and the habitual revelation of thought. . . . Speech is human nature itself."[8] "The mentality of mankind and the language of mankind created each other. If we like to assume the rise of language as a given fact, then it is not going too far to say that the souls of men are the gift from language to mankind. The account of the sixth day [sc. of creation] should be written, He gave them speech, and they became souls."[9] I leave it to you to decide whether Whitehead's proposal for rewriting the Genesis account of man's creation does not in fact fit astonishingly closely what is said and meant in that account. What should be clear is that his one-substance metaphysics in no way obscures "the difference of man and the difference it makes"—to use the title of Mortimer Adler's book of a few years ago—although, quite unlike Adler, Whitehead sharply challenges the traditional assumption that man can be treated as more than a mere means, and thus as an end in himself, only if the rest of earth's creatures cannot.

I have one concluding comment. In the course of this paper I have either asserted or implied that there is no one process philosophy but only several process philosophies. Thus, in trying to indicate the significance of process philosophy for the new Christian theology of nature that is now urgently called for, I have appealed solely to Whitehead's version of process philosophy. The reason for this is not that many other versions of process philosophy do not make, more or less consistently, the same points that Whitehead allows one to make. The reason, rather, is that Whitehead, on the whole, is a good deal freer from the man-centeredness of the Western theological-philosophical tradition, which still finds expression even in some versions of process philosophy—or, at least, philosophical-theological speculations that are in certain respects similar to Whitehead's. I am thinking here especially of Pierre Teilhard de Chardin, who, along with Whitehead, probably enjoys the greatest audience of any of the thinkers in the recent process tradition, especially in Roman Catholic cultural and religious circles. Perhaps because Whitehead is, above all, a metaphysician, whereas Teilhard remains, after all, a mystically oriented speculative cosmologist, the latter still has a conception of nature and of man's place and role in it that I find remarkably, not to say, incredibly, anthropocentric. His theme is the ancient theme of all speculative cosmologies—ultimate origins and ultimate ends—and the picture of cosmic evolution he projects is, in effect, simply a generalization, which falls short of achieving strict metaphysical generality, of the biblical history of salvation, with creation somewhere in the remote past and the last things somewhere in the remote future. Not surprisingly, "the phenomenon of man" for Teilhard has a unique place, not only among the forms of life known to us on this planet, but among the entirety of created beings. Indeed, if I read him correctly, such justification as the rest of creation can finally claim is merely the indirect justification that derives from its being the necessary prehistory and cosmic setting of specifically human history. The creation generally is finally fulfilled only in and through God's supernatural donation of himself to mankind in Christ. "The whole movement of material growth in the universe is ultimately directed toward spirit, and the whole movement of spiritual growth is ultimately directed toward Christ."[10] In other words, on Teilhard's view, *cosmogenesis* is for the sake of *biogenesis* is for the sake of *anthropogenesis* is for the sake of *Christogenesis*. On Whitehead's view, by contrast, such man-centeredness, even on this grand cosmological scale, is undercut. He rejects the kind of eschatology which envisages, in Tennyson's words, "that far-off divine event/To which the whole creation moves" as "a fallacious conception of the universe."[11] And his own conception of what is ultimate allows for no such anthropocentrism as is typical of Teilhard. "The present type of order in the world has arisen from an unimaginable past, and it will find its grave in an unimaginable future. There remains the inexhaustible realm of abstract forms, and creativity, with its shifting character ever determined afresh by its own creatures, and God, upon whose wisdom all forms of order depend."[12] Perhaps the most serious issue a new Christian theology of nature has to face is whether the essential claims of the Christian witness of faith can be expressed in terms so completely purified as Whitehead's are of all anthropocentrism. One may urge, in any event, that it is only in some such terms that we can be wholly freed from the basic philosophical and theological presuppositions which are not entirely unconnected with our ecological crisis—that crisis which makes new reflection on nature one of the urgent theological tasks of the hour.

NOTES

1. *Is It Too Late? A Theology of Ecology* (Beverly Hills, Calif.: Bruce, 1972), p. 87.

2. Ibid.

3. *Process and Reality: An Essay in Cosmology* (New York: Macmillan Co., 1929), p. 252; *Adventures of Ideas* (New York: Macmillan Co., 1933), p. 284.

4. *Modes of Thought* (New York: Macmillan Co., 1938), pp. 231 f.

5. *Process and Reality*, p. 32.

6. *Modes of Thought*, pp. 37 f.

7. Ibid., pp. 104 f.

8. Ibid., pp. 51 f.

9. Ibid., p. 57.

10. *Mon Univers*, in *Science et Christ* (Paris: Seuil, 1965), p. 96.

11. *Process and Reality*, p. 169.

12. *Religion in the Making* (New York: Macmillan Co., 1926), p. 160.

THE RATIONALIST DENIAL OF JEWISH TRADITION IN PHILO

SAMUEL SANDMEL

I ASSUME in this paper that some possible readers are not specialists in Philo, and I therefore begin with some words of introduction. Philo's dates are often given as 20 B.C. to 40 A.D. He was a native of Alexandria; he alludes to a trip to Judea, but how long he was there we do not know, nor do we know if that was his only visit. Apart from a few treatises, such as *Against Flaccus* and the *Legation to Caius* (these reflecting his sturdy Jewish loyalties), and such as *That Every Good Man Is Free* and *On the Comtemplative Life,* everything that he wrote is related to Scripture, almost exclusively the Pentateuch. These writings on Scripture have been divided by modern analysts into three groups. One body, "Questions and Solutions to Genesis and Exodus," is accurately named. Philo asks what a passage means, and then gives an answer. These questions and answers are, in a sense, preliminary notes containing materials utilized and repeated in the other two groups, which are a series of full-blown essays, each bearing a title. One of these latter two groups is called the "Allegory." It consists of a number of treatises whose shape and form are dictated by a series of connected scriptural verses; the treatises in the other, called the "Exposition," are on topics, and lack the initial scriptural passage which invariably opens an essay in the "Allegory." For example, *On the Migration of Abraham*, part of the "Allegory," begins by citing Genesis 12:1–3; *Concerning Abraham*, lacking a scriptural beginning, is in the "Exposition." Let it be noted that the "Exposition" utilizes allegory quite as fully as does the "Allegory."

A few words need to be devoted to what allegory is. This rhetorical device, quite ancient among the Greeks, was applied by the Stoics in their approach to Homer. Its manner is to read into an ancient text a meaning not actually there. Allegory, both before and after Philo, is a strategem on the part of an interpreter of adulated literature either to get around passages which to him are difficult or embarrassing or both, or else to justify a freedom essential for his expansive creativity. In the case of Philo, allegory served as a means both for escaping from disquieting scriptural problems and also for reading Platonism and Stoicism into the biblical text. An effect of the use of allegory, by Philo and others, was to shift some item in Scripture from being a matter of ancient history, that is , a dynamic event of long ago, into a contemporaneous, static philosophical or quasi-philosophical matter. For example, Philo asserts that we need have no interest in Abraham's migration from one place to another unless it was a spiritual journey which we too can make; this spiritual journey was a departure from the error and atheism of astrology and an arrival into introspection, and then the resultant momentous discovery of the existence of God.[1]

This liquidation of history ought to impress the modern analyst with Philo's unique talent to carry water on at least two shoulders. Seeming to deny that Abraham actually left a place named Ur to arrive at a place actually named Charran, Philo will proceed to reestablish history in the sense that his allegorical Abraham was a historical sage, of a given time and place, who historically did abandon astrology, and historically did come to the knowledge of this one God.

But Philo can write in such a way as to persuade, or at least half-persuade, us that he is totally liquidating history. Thus the rivalry, if we may call it that, between Sarah and Hagar,[2] prompts him to an essay, *On Mating for the Sake of Erudition*, in which he sets forth the assets and liabilities of the ancient liberal arts curriculum, the so-called encyclical studies, symbolized by Hagar, contrasted with true wisdom, Sarah, and implying that true wisdom must always "punish," that is , discipline, the encyclical studies and their student, as the Sarah of Genesis disciplined Hagar and Ishmael. But Philo closes this treatise by the plainest sort of denial that Sarah and Hagar are historical persons. Scripture, he tells us, has no interest in telling us about backyard quarrels of mere women.

If we had only this passage, we could with justice conclude that Philo really means to liquidate early Hebrew history. But it is possible that either a momentary, passing enthusiasm or something else has led him into a statement he does not really mean, at least does not mean in the form in which he actually makes it.

Now to the core of my paper. Greek Jews gave to the Pentateuch the name *Nomos,* the Law. Greek Jews lived in the center of three concentric circles of law. The inner circle was Jewish law, both the scriptural and, in the case of Philo, some Alexandrian analogue to what we mean in the case of rabbinic Judaism by the term *halacha.*[3] Around this circle of Jewish law there was that of local hellenistic law, and, in turn, around the local hellenistic there was the over-arching imperial Roman law.

Now, however unique aspects of Pentateuchal law may be, there is a sense in which all legal systems contain analogous materials, such as a distinction between theft and burglary or between manslaughter and murder. To state this in another way, at points Jewish law, on the one hand, and the hellenistic and the Roman, on the other, overlap. What, then, is the unique virtue of Jewish law?

If its virtue might be defended as its being a product of God's revelation, we then discover that Philo abstains from making so bald a claim, since among other reasons, this would unduly smack of history; Sinai could seem, indeed, like an irrational legend, and potentially as objectionable as the Olympian myths. Philo chooses a way different from asserting a simple, literal divine revelation of laws.

He struggles to defend Genesis, notably narration, as suitable to *nomos*, that is, to law, by ascribing to it the Stoic notion of the law of nature, the unwritten concept of law accessible to the mind of the gifted men who rise above sense and passion.[4]

In using the Stoic item, Philo is quite eloquent about the patriarchs, Abraham, Isaac, and Jacob, and their attainment of living by the law of nature. All gifted people, Jew or Gentile, can potentially rise to the level of living by the law of nature, provided they possess *orthos logos*, impeccably correct dialectic. But to progress by this means not only restricts progress to the elite few, it also imposes great burdens of dialectic on even these. Hence, God graciously made it easier for man, this through the laws which begin in Exodus 20, and hence men can rely on these laws, instead of on their capacity for unassailable dialectic. The laws in Exodus through Deuteronomy are records of what Abraham, Isaac, and Jacob had done; he who obeyed the Mosaic laws was thereby living exactly as the three patriarchs had lived. People of lower mentality, in obeying the Mosaic laws, were living like the patriarchs but doing so only by coincidence. Better minds, adept at allegory, saw in their observance of the Mosaic laws a dimension of the inherent spiritual significance which was lost on the crowd, the ordinary people.[5]

The Stoics had distinguished between the unwritten law of nature and "particular" laws, the latter being the written royal decrees and legislative enactments of the city-states. The particular laws were at best an imitation of, or a substitution for, the law of nature. To turn now to some of our own terminology, the law of nature we would designate as primary, the particular laws only as secondary. For Philo to denominate the Mosaic laws, beginning in Exodus 20, as particular laws amounted both to his ascribing only a secondary importance to them, and also to the startling observation that he puts them in the same category as the decrees and enactments of the city-states.

Does Philo really mean to assign the Mosaic laws to this secondary position? Or was it his putting Scripture into a Procrustean Stoic bed that accounts for this anomaly? True, he struggles with the implications of this strange assignment in that he gives two reasons for holding to the superiority of the Mosaic laws to other particular laws, namely, that the Mosaic laws are everywhere the same, but when one moves from one city-state to another, the Greek laws change; and, second, the Mosaic laws are eternal, but the laws of the city-states are subject to repeal, innovation, and alteration. Accordingly, the Mosaic laws are unquestionably the best of the particular laws,[6] and of all the particular laws they are the most consistent with nature. Yet particular laws they nevertheless remain. Parenthetically, Philo's way is, as it were, the opposite of the rabbis'; the latter portray the patriarchs as pre-Mosaic observers of the Mosaic laws, bringing Abraham, as it were, up to the level of Moses, while Philo's effort is to bring the Mosaic laws up to the level of Abraham.[7]

Again, Philo informs us that Moses never commands. Rather, Moses instructs and encourages. We who are reared with the phrase *Torah tzivah lanu Moshe* ("Moses commanded the Torah to us") might find this startling. We should recall, though, that for Philo, reason, i.e., rationalism, is its own persuader, this by virtue of the very nature of reason. Since the particular laws of Moses are reasonable, they commend themselves without at all requiring the force of commandment to become commendable. A sage observes the laws not for the reason that Moses had commanded them but simply because it is reasonable to do so.

We need now to advert to a complicating and complicated factor. In Philo's allegory, the biblical personalities become philosophical abstractions. Abraham is the trait, or the capacity, to learn, Isaac is intuition, and Jacob is practice. All of us who are more than dolts possess aspects of these human traits. What is Moses allegorically? In answer, he is the logos.

Let me here do no more than briefly indicate what Philo means by this tortured and torturing term. Logos, in one sense, is the highest point to which man's mind can take him as the mind moves out from the routine of daily existence and progresses toward God; logos is also the lowest point to which God descends in graciously moving toward man. God himself is transcendent; logos, so we may say, is the immanent aspect of the transcendent God. Or we may say that logos is the rational activity of God within man's world. So much in greatest brevity.

The Jewish ancestor of logos is the Torah-Hochmah equation; the Greek ancestor is *sophia, epistēmē,* and the like. Logos, to try again, is the revealed and revealing wisdom of God. And Moses, allegorically, is the logos of God.

Now, if Moses is allegorically the logos, then the Mosaic particular laws are not quite the same as the purely human enactments of the rulers of the city-states. Since in a sense logos is the revealed and revealing wisdom of God, then in a sense the laws of Moses are a product of revelation.

In saying this Philo is for the most part within proper Stoicism. A Stoic could feel quite at home with Philo's pattern, though he might not be ready to concede that the Jewish Moses and the Stoic logos could be truly identical. Perhaps we might put it in this way, that Philo the Jew is a good Stoic, but it is hard to see how a Gentile Stoic could become a Philonic Jew.

By his stoicism (with a generous helping of Platonism) Philo manages both to deny literal revelation to the Mosaic laws and obliquely to affirm their divine origin.

Now we may query: Is it legitimate to conclude that, differentiating between philosophy and religion, philosophically Philo is moved at points to deny what religiously he affirms? Do other Jewish philosophers do this, too? Is this procedure in any way similar to the practice of close and cherished friends (and to some extent, though less, my own) of academically repudiating what religiously they preserve and observe? Are there Jewish scholars who are personally *mehadrin min hamehadrin* ("scrupulously observant") but whose researches and publications smack of pure heterodoxy? Are there scholarly rabbis who at a Tuesday evening Bible class are quite Wellhausenite, but on Shabbas morning deliver sermons as if on the premise of *Torah min hashamayim* ("the heavenly origin of the Bible")? I do not intend the slightest scorn in noting these possibilities. Rather, I intend to thereby make what seems to me the important point, that a Jewish or a Christian academician, in utilizing the Greek legacy, can find himself making philosophical assertions in all earnestness and conviction that he personally repudiates religiously. Respecting Philo, the case is, I believe, that his explanations of religious phenomena are invariably Grecian; the religious intuitions and perceptions which require explanation are, invariably, Jewish. Philo seems to affirm religiously what he seems to deny philosophically.

NOTES

1. See my *Philo's Place in Judaism*, pp. 105, 111–12, and 144. See his treatise *On the Virtues* 211–16, and "Abraham's Knowledge of the Existence of God," *Harvard Theological Review* 44 (1951): 137–39.

2. See *Philo's Place in Judaism*, p. 155, especially n. 250. The passage is in *De Congressu* 158–60 and QG III, 24–26. The biblical basis is Gen. 16:9.

3. On the question of the possible relationship and dependency of Philonic and Judean *halacha*, see *Philo's Place in Judaism*, pp. 9 and 109, for references to the literature.

4. The subtitle to *De Abrahamo* is "The Life of the Sage Made Perfect through Instruction; or, The First Book on Unwritten Laws." Philo begins *De Abrahamo* with the statement that he is not yet ready to discuss the particular laws, which are only copies; he must begin with those that are *katholikotera* ("general"), archetypes of the copies. In Philo's exposition, the patriarchs are themselves *nomoi empsychoi*, "laws embodied in men."

5. Respecting the laws themselves. Philo distinguishes between their literal import, which he calls the "mystery of Aaron," and the "mystery of Moses," the allegorical meaning. See *Philo's Place in Judaism*, pp. 102 and 197.

6. See ibid., p. 197; cf. *Migration of Abraham* 89–93.

7. See *Philo's Place in Judaism*, p. 108.

EDUCATING THE MENTAL HEALTH RESEARCHER FOR POTENTIAL DEVELOPMENT IN MAN

DAVID SHAKOW

WHEN I initially prepared the talk which I have modified for the present paper, I did not have in mind only the person to whose memory it was dedicated. It was also an implicit tribute to those persons important in my development who embodied the principles and spirit of what I was attempting to express: those I had come to know indirectly through the professional literature, and those who had been my colleagues or other direct professional associates. One of these was Levi Olan, a friend who, during the more than three decades I have known him, has been concerned in so many ways with important social issues and the encouragement of potential growth in man.

It was originally through William James's influence that I had—even in precollege days—become greatly intrigued by the problems of psychopathology and mental health. As time went on, I came more and more to realize the vast gaps of knowledge in this area. During this period, I had also been particularly impressed by the implications of James's essay on "The Energies of Men."[1] (pp. 229–64) This sagacious essay was prepared in the first years of this century for his presidential address to the American

Philosophical Association. James closed with two points he considered of paramount importance. One dealt with the possible extent of the latent powers of man; the other, with the various keys for unlocking these powers and making them available in diverse individuals. He believed these principles to dominate the whole problem of individual and national education. James's tenets, indeed his entire essay, have relevance for mental health, as well as for general education. Over the years, I have found the two themes of mental health and the energies of man to converge, to intertwine, and even to contain elements that are clearly part of the same problem.

In my early personal relationships with distinguished persons in psychiatry and psychology—McDougall, Prince, Campbell, Wells, Hill, and many others—and in my acquaintance with the giants of the literature, I was profoundly struck by the amount of ignorance they admitted; this despite the fact that I view myself as fundamentally an optimist, not an iconoclast or a pessimist in search of the negative! With experience I became ever more aware of the complexities of psychopathology and, necessarily, of the human nature that underlies it. The unanswered problems seemed boundless. As an individual, I continued to accept the importance of providing immediate help to persons in distress, but as a professional, my recognition of the need to acquire more knowledge through study grew. I became convinced that the slow, investigative road was in the end the surer. This feeling may even have played an unconscious role in my choice of psychology rather than psychiatry as a profession, because the former was not faced so forcefully with the injunction to help—a principle so integral to medical training.

So many facets of mental health call for study that even if one limits oneself to training, and for the purposes of this essay, to the area closest to my own central interests, *research* training, one must concede that a large expanse of ignorance still remains. With that in mind, I will focus on a consideration of some of the principles I believe to be involved in the preparation of persons directed toward contributing knowledge to the field of mental health through research.

The topic of research training evokes a pertinent challenge. How can we bring ourselves to emphasize investigation when we are faced with the crying needs of the field as a whole? It is especially difficult to ignore the insistent pressures from the public for immediate action. Such demands are not only helpful in keeping the field alert by telling us where it hurts, but further, by impelling us to justify our recommendations as to how public (or private) funds should be spent. But it is just here that the more experienced, more sophisticated members of the relevant social forces—the professionals in the field—come in. A compelling rationale for the existence of a profession, it seems to me, is to provide the longer-range vision represented by an ability to discriminate among conflicting values, and with reason and tact to help direct a field toward its ultimately greatest social contribution. A special part of this responsibility lies in clarifying and persistently reaffirming the importance of, and the need for, research.

We should not forget that research has two aspects, both of great importance to the development of any field. There is, of course, the *primary search for new knowledge*—whether basic or applied—which is directed toward solving, or at least alleviating, problems. The other aspect, though closely bound to the research for new knowledge, is concerned with the *evaluation of existing knowledge*. Too often, in the press of meeting immediate problems, we neglect what is almost as important as the doing itself. I refer to the evaluation techniques for determining the *effectiveness* of what we are doing. This is not a simple problem. It is easy enough to find naive and superficial rating scales or other measurements—devices essentially irrelevant for getting at the subtle changes with which we are usually concerned. Much research has yet to be done on developing sensitive, sophisticated evaluative methods. We cannot avoid this equal obligation to society—except in dire emergencies—to evaluate *what* we are doing while we *do* what we are doing.

Goals in Training for Research

We are deluged today with the theme of human

potentialities—peak experiences, Esalen, expanding awareness through drugs and other devices. My rather conservative nature rebels somewhat at becoming associated with this trend to "overall." I am fortified, to some extent, however, by two facts: first, my own long-time and early interest in human potentialities; and second, my recognition of the complexity of human nature.

These parallel views, which obviously derive from James, are expressed in practically all his writings, including "The Energies of Men." Further evidence is to be found in an unpublished letter in my possession that James wrote to a woman who had sent him a reprint of an ecstatic article she had written about ESP for the *Forum*. He sympathized with her feelings, but added, "I tremble at your enthusiasm." At the same time, in his inimitably gentle way, he indicated how slow progress in this area was, and how difficult proof was to obtain.

In his essay James dealt not only with the extent of man's energies and the ways of making them available, but he indicated why he held these to be the central problems of individual and national education. I have done a little research on James's essay. I have examined the internal evidence in the two versions of his paper* and have studied what little I have been able to find in contemporary Jamesian material. In the attempt to figure out what James had in mind, I conclude that his concern was with the untapped wells of *energy* available to us, the second and third (and even fourth) "winds" about which he speaks, and which, he points out, we so rarely employ in our daily life.

Thus his emphasis appears to be centered on a *drive* concept—on the affective-conative, motivational, striking, "will" aspect of personality. Although I recognize the overwhelming importance of will, I see this as an unnecessary limitation on the range of human expression. It seems to me equally important to extend the notion he applied to energy to

---

*In 1907 a popular version of James's talk appeared under the title "The Powers of Men."

the *cognitive* side as well. For I believe that parallel with the untapped range of energy capacities, man has a similar range of untapped cognitive capacities. For our purposes, it is useful to keep "second" and "third" winds, and layers of untapped cognitive function apart. They are on the whole separable, and do have different theoretical implications, though ultimately, of course, these two aspects of personality are closely related and become integrated in such a fashion as to make them difficult to separate. At one point James himself seems to realize this when he talks of these changes in energy level as producing "extra-ordinary qualitative results."[2]

So the term "potential" includes for me *both* energies and cognitive capacities. I relate this to training for research because I believe we should be concerned with developing researchers who would be interested in determining man's range of cognitive potential as well as the correlative range of energy potential. They should then be interested in studying ways of releasing the expression of both kinds of potentialities to their fullest. Such a program would have integrally built into it the central notions of individuality and diversity on the one hand, and flexibility on the other—principles that are such characteristic Jamesian hallmarks.

In proposing these goals, I recognize that they are indeed lofty goals, high aspirations to strive for, but I have never believed in shooting low. Nor do I believe them to be unattainable goals. I am convinced that such potentialities exist and that they can be tapped to a far greater degree than they have been. Certain amounts of these potentiality areas are probably not intended for ordinary day-to-day use. There *must* be reserves which nature sets aside for use only in times of great emergency, such as those of extreme physical or psychological danger. But in between what we characteristically use and what we do not, tremendous areas of untapped, potentially accessible resources lie fallow.

Nevertheless, in accepting low levels of performance more or less unquestioningly, both with respect to the effort we put into our activities and the range of our potential capacities, have we not been suffering from what James called "habit-neurosis"? There are, of course, obstacles to these achievements, as well as forces which favor their expression. The handicaps to tapping them may be so great that we may have to settle for only a partial reduction in the present limitations on the expression of potentiality. With this reservation, the problem that faces us is how to overcome such handicaps and avail ourselves of the untapped resources. Part of my presentation will therefore be devoted to a proposed program for introducing training in this task into our development of mental health researchers.

Content of Program

It appears best to consider the training of researchers in a conservative context, in the sense of focusing on the training of those being prepared for the core professions we commonly accept as involved in mental health. Except for psychology, I am, of course, in no position to make specific recommendations to other professions as to how to train their students; each group will attempt to develop the most competent professionals it can. I see my task, rather, as that of indicating ways in which this training can be amplified and complemented through the introduction of research attitudes and methodology.

Taken across the board, what does this imply? Essentially, it calls for fostering in the student, whatever his group, a questioning, critical attitude. I mean, of course, critical not of the general goals of research for mental health, but rather, critical and ready to raise questions about whether what is generally accepted, or what he is doing, is the best way of achieving the sought-for goals. This calls for the acquisition, among other qualities, of a humility that recognizes how much ignorance still characterizes the field.

Our training in research should fundamentally comprise two areas: one substantive, and the other methodological. The level of difficulty and degree of complexity of the content and organization of each area would necessarily be determined by the student's background, profession, and stage of advancement. In the *substantive* area, I note three kinds of training: in personality principles, in real-life situations, and in real clinical situations. In the *methodological* area, I would include two kinds of training: in observation, and in specific research methodology.

Substantive Training Areas

The program on the nature and development of personality would aim, whenever possible in the context of actual life situations and concrete case material, at producing in the student an apperceptive mass which has incorporated the five principles basic to the understanding of personality: the genetic, the cryptic, the dynamic, the psychobiological, and the psychosocial.

The *genetic* principle acknowledges the role of continuity in the development of the individual's personality characteristics—the significance of earlier influences on present manifestations of his personality. The *cryptic* principle recognizes that unconscious and preconscious factors act as crucial determiners of behavior; that behavior has, besides the obvious conscious motivations, further motivations that are not conscious. The student would learn that these latter motivations are rarely perceptible to the person himself, and frequently, except through the use of special techniques, not even to the trained observer. The *dynamic* principle states that behavior is drive-determined, that behind behavior lie certain innate or acquired impelling forces. The *psychobiological* principle holds that the personality is integral and indivisible, that there is a pervasive interrelationship between psyche and soma. This involves the acceptance of an organismic concept of total, rather than segmental, personality. The *psychosocial* principle recognizes the integration of the person and his social environment as a unit. It states that behavior is expressed as individual response within a social context, and that *both* the individual and his environment are important in the determination of personality and conduct.

The second substantive area would involve the student in as

many normal settings, both adequate and deprived, as possible—in home, community, school, playground, etc.—so that he may acquire experience with a broad range of normal individual and social behavior. Another aspect of this substantive area would involve the student in experience with varieties of clinical situations, from the minor aberrations of personality through the most complex of the psychoses. I cannot overemphasize the importance of both of these kinds of field work for developing the mental health workers we seek. In many ways I consider extensive "clinical" experience—experience with human beings in a diversity of human settings—as the very foundation of a sound program of education.

Methodological Training Areas

On the *methodological* side, two major areas of training are indicated. The first would provide varied experience with the different types of observation; the second, experience with more specific research methodology, in part based on the training in observation.

Observation is essential because of the ubiquity of human *variability*. Significant though the problem is in the biological sciences, variability is an even more profound problem in the behavioral sciences, which consistently call for the observation of human beings by other human beings. There is marked intra- and interindividual variability in the observed, and almost as great a variability of both kinds in the observer as instrument. Since so much of mental health work depends on observation, our researchers must become good observers of the whole spectrum of human behavior.

I distinguish four major types of observation: objective observation, participant observation, empathic observation, and self-observation.

Objective observation involves the careful description of the impact on the observed of those impinging internal and external forces—physical, psychological, and social—that lead to his behaving the way he does. Such observations are those of the naturalist; they are made from a point outside the subject and his situation. The observer is not directly involved with the subject; he only observes his overt behavior. It is particularly important for the observer to become sensitive to the more transient, nonverbal behavioral aspects, such as body movement and facial expression. Because the subject frequently hides behind words (as do the rest of us), such perceptivity is essential. Objective observation plays a significant role as well in the process of building up the "computer" capability of the student. In the diagnostic realm, because so many of the cues used by the expert clinician are below the level of communication, he often depends for his evaluations on automatic, computerlike activity stemming from his accumulated experiences.

The second kind of observation, *participant observation*, implies a distinctly more intimate relationship between the observer and the observed, for in this situation both are interacting within a group. To the observer falls the difficult task not only of making objective observations, but also of determining how his role as a participant in the group modifies the situation. He needs, as well, to evaluate the effect that the very act of observing has on the observed and the observation. The group may consist of just two, the subject and the student, as occurs in one of the most common forms of this kind of interaction—history-taking. In mental health settings, aside from history-taking, it is most strikingly represented in psychotherapy, especially in group psychotherapy situations in which the psychotherapist is both observer and therapist.

The third kind of observation, *emphatic observation*, is a particularly important one for mental health workers. It involves the observer's attempt to feel with the patient, to try to understand how he feels about himself, his family, and his illness. Whether these feelings be realistic or unrealisitic, they are essential for understanding the patient's difficulties.

The fourth kind of observation is *self-observation*, the student's effort to understand his own feelings and attitudes. Here he asks himself why he behaves the way he does—why, for instance, he is so anxious with one patient and so calm with another. Such self-knowledge would seem indispensable in the field of mental health, where the worker is constantly called upon for sensitivity to the psychological and social aspects of others' disturbances. Nowhere else, perhaps, is it as important to be aware of the dangers that lie in projecting one's own difficulties onto others.

In discussing these four kinds of observation, I am emphasizing techniques for learning by experiencing, as opposed to learning by listening. Real-life learning techniques, however, carry with them certain hazards. On the one hand, they may disturb the validity of the observations, and on the other, they may develop self-consciousness or exaggerated introspectiveness. Such hazards call for caution on the part of preceptors and their students, and for careful consideration of ways to reduce these negative aspects.

Implementation of Program

How should an educational program set for so many different levels of expertness, background, and variety of disciplines be implemented? It is a tall order, made even taller since we must at the same time keep before us the primary principle stated earlier: to take advantage, in our students as well as in our clients, of as much of their energy expression and cognitive capacity as possible.

I can merely take a stab at outlining a suitable program for the most advanced levels. I assume that persons directing programs of this type will adapt them to the levels of the groups that are technically less prepared. At least we might lay out the principles of attack, sketch a sample experimental program, and trust that the trials and errors arising in the course of its implementation will teach us how to carry on from there.

The two major areas of content we have already suggested—the methodological and the substantive—are the ones that call for more detailed description. But in their exposition we must be concerned with the *context* of implementation as well as with the content. By context I refer, of course, to the educational principles, the teaching methods we must follow to bring about the most effective education in these content areas.

Methodology

On the *methodological* side, the aim is to develop the researcher as a competent and precise device for describing and evaluating the persons he is studying. He goes about this in two ways: first, by making of himself a refined and accurate instrument for this purpose; and second, by acquiring techniques and procedures that will further aid him in obtaining dependable research data. Training in observation seems to be a reasonable way of achieving self-refinement as an instrument, since almost all of mental health activity depends on the description and evaluation of complexities of general behavior, feelings, and symptoms.

The Teaching of Observation. It is important that before students begin to work extensively in the field, they have fairly substantial preliminary training in *naturalistic observation and report.* These are the factors on which diagnosis and therapy are so integrally based.* These observations should, in general, be carried out on those persons who present relatively milder problems. Their behavior and feelings, as well as their symptoms, are closer to the student's own and already sufficiently complex for him to deal with at this early stage of training. The quality of the training can be much improved through the use of one-way screens and paired observers in settings where individuals and groups are under observation in both free and controlled situations. Constant checking of observers' reports against each other, against supervisors' observations, and even against tape and video recordings, should be part of the routine. Both in diagnostic study and in reporting, insistence on succinctness and accurate terminology are essential. Early training in observation also helps to point up the dangers that inhere in acquiring technical terms too soon—a step so seductive to the neophyte. Premature knowledge of such terminology frequently serves as a barrier to the accurate observation of the conditions with which the student is concerned.

---

*For those interested in what training in observation really entails, I would recommend the Harvard geologist Shaler's autobiographical account of his tutelage under Agassiz.[3] (pp. 98–99)

In *participant observation* the difficulties of naturalistic observation are augmented, especially in relation to the data, and in the effect on what is observed. Like any reported observations, the data that become available are limited by the capacity of the human observer as a reporting instrument. No matter how able human beings may be as conceptualizers, they are limited in how much they can initially grasp, in how much they can remember of what they do grasp, and in how much and how well they can report even the slight amount they have grasped and remembered.

The participant-observation situation places even greater strictures upon the reported data, since one depends here on a participant-observer whose participation is special and likely to be extensive. Distortions, both of omission and commission, arising from the situation itself, as well as from the personality characteristics and problems of the observer, undoubtedly enter here far more than they do in the naturalistic observation setting. It is for these reasons that the training techniques described earlier for naturalistic observation must be provided even more deliberately and intensively in participant-observation settings.

In the case of *emphatic observation* we are concerned with insight into the nature of another person's characteristics and difficulties as he himself sees them. Such insight and understanding are essential in the mental health worker's armamentarium. The student must learn to simultaneously meet the opposing demands of identification and objectivity entailed in working with human problems. Toward this end, he should be provided with opportunities to participate in role-playing and psychodrama exercises. On one occasion he may be asked to play the part of a person with a certain type of difficulty; on another, to adopt the role of the helping person. In this way the student has an opportunity to gain a greater appreciation of the "feeling" of being disturbed, as well as to obtain a kind of "experience" in dealing with various disorders. Despite questions which have been raised about these approaches, I have found them, when taken seriously by the student, to be effective devices preparatory to actual work with patients. Audio and video tapings of some of these sessions might well be used as the basis for group discussion by students and a supervisor. I have found such group discussions to afford one of the most stimulating and creative opportunities for learning.

The fourth kind of observation, *self-observation*, is important because the subjective feelings of the observer are particularly problematical when dealing with motivation. For here one's own biases, affects, and problems—frequently different from the patient's only in intensity—color the material provided by the client. So persistent has this problem been that those engaged in clinical psychiatry and in the behavioral sciences have come to recognize self-evaluation as a prerequisite for their work. Many have undergone some form of psychoanalysis, a course I would recommend for those in the more responsible research positions. For most students, however, short periods of self-evaluation may suffice. Whatever the nature and depth of the chosen procedure, the self-examination should be carried out under the competent guidance of experienced persons. The detailed case supervision in social work training might be applicable to many students in the field of mental health, with the aim of examining and working through the student's egocentric attitudes in his dealings with a particular patient.

Research Methodology. The second area of methodological training, though based fundamentally on the training in observation, is that more directly related to research methodology. Obviously the range here is great, and usually determined by the nature of the student's specific discipline. The general principles common to all researchers, such as accuracy and reliability of report, would presumably have been acquired largely through the training in observation. The specifics of the particular disciplinary techniques set up to yield dependable data, the experimental and statistical controls necessary to support them, and other substantive and methodological details, remain the concrete problem of the educators in each of the disciplines—from the biological through the social.

Substantive

The Teaching of Personality and the Human Potential. Along with the methodological area is the other major area of content, the *substantive*, which centers around personality, its development and its expressions. I think of this as constituted of two closely related programs, one of which would emphasize the development of the normal personality in the context of the five major principles considered earlier, in combination with the life experience and associated field clinical courses. Using this program on the course of personality growth as a core, I would then build around it another course, at first dealing separately and in detail with the principles relating to the potentialities of man in his motivational and cognitive functioning, and finally dealing with both these aspects of functioning in integrated fashion. A program of this kind, with its complementary lectures, seminars, readings, and field work, should go far to impress upon the student what James was driving at when he considered the "energies of men" to "dominate the whole problem of individual and national education."[1] (p. 263)

We are all aware of the emphasis on the positive during the past few decades, with the accompanying negative attitude manifested toward anything which smacks of disorder (a trend I pointed out in an earlier paper).[4] Thus, "mental disease" has been replaced by "mental health," an understandable and reasonable change. But for some this change has apparently not been sufficient. We have had dinned into our ears a Madison Avenue–type slogan of *"positive* mental health," as if there was a *negative* mental health—as if being healthy wasn't good enough. And in recent days this trend has had hitched onto it a bandwagon, a fad of sentience and "groupiness" onto which so many have leaped.

Having been brought up in the Jamesian tradition that accepts wholeheartedly the normality/abnormality continuum,* I find

---

*Phenomena are best understood when placed within their series, studied in their germ and their overripe decay, and compared with their exaggerated and degenerated kindred."[5](p.382)

myself rather troubled by this one-sided emphasis, which appears to me to gloss over the realities of the full range of human nature. It is in this kind of context that I present an outline of a program of study which deals with human potentialities when seen as part of the totality of human functioning—not the exaggerations represented in certain aspects of such movements as Esalen, psychedelism, ESP, mysticism, Eastern philosophies, and madness as health and liberation*—the exaggerations which emphasize effect at the expense of cognition, casualness at the expense of commitment, groupism at the expense of individuality, "emoting" at the expense of acting, and the relatively rare, isolated experience at the expense of the common wisdom.

Let me give you at least a glimpse of what I would include in such a program. In an introductory section dealing historically with the two principles, I would consider the relationship of the conflicting trends of freedom and constriction as characteristic of personality. I would consider next the very strong obstacles in human nature to the expression of its range of potentialities, points of the kind my colleague Paul MacLean has brought out in his outstanding experiments and theorizing about reptilian and paleomammalian brains in their relation to the neomammalian.[8] (pp. 336–49) I would then go into a consideration of the positive indications for the existence of these trends of freedom. I would point out the evidence for the "excitements, ideas, and efforts" James spoke of as motivating forces for increased energy,[2] as manifested in such dedicated groups as the Oneida Community, the kibbutzim, modern Mainland Chinese culture, and

---

*This is brought to the fore in David Cooper's introduction to Foucault's *Madness and Civilization*,[6] but one is also left with something of this impression after reading much of R. D. Laing's writings. No matter how much exception one may take to its generality, it is important to the field of mental health that Laing and his group have made their point so strongly. (Albert Goldman's portrait of Laing in *Psychotherapy and Social Science Review* 5, no. 9 [July 26, 1971], does, however, raise questions!) An enlightened discussion of insanity as health in its relationship to the issue of authenticity is to be found in Lionel Trilling's recent Charles Eliot Norton Lectures at Harvard (see especially p. 166–72).[7]

Nader's Raiders; the near triumph over insurmountable obstacles by individuals such as Scott in his battle for life in the Antarctic (so poignantly described in his own diary[9] and in Cherry-Garrard's *Worst Journey in the World*[10]); the challenge of deep and sensitive psychotherapy, as reflected in Sechehaye's Renee,[11] Milner's Susan,[12] D'Ambrosio's Laura,[13] and Axline's Dibs;[14] the victory over genetic difficulty of a Nigel Hunt,[15] and over physical handicap by a Helen Keller[16] or a Margaret Bourke-White;[17] the overcoming of concentration camp experiences of persons like Bettelheim[18] and Frankl.[19] I would deal not only with such instances of unusual spurts of energy and with the uncovering of hidden capacities, but would also consider why so many of these spurts, though not all, are effective for only limited periods, and others so much longer-lasting, making the attempt to evaluate the factors, temporary or permanent, involved in these phenomena.

As part of the program, I would examine in detail the many individual cases, mostly from the literature (some of which I have just mentioned), as well as experimental work on behavior under marked stress, as in sensory deprivation and starvation, and the Neal Miller type of research on biofeedback and the conscious control of autonomic functions.[20] I would also encourage the students to participate in studies of underprivileged environments and experimental growth environments. As another part of the program, I would examine as well the exciting new developments in primary education in the so-called open education described by Featherstone[21] and developed further by him in recent issues of the *New Republic*.[22]* As part of a reading course, I would include, among others, the classic cases described in *Triumph Over Odds*,[23] *Out of the Depths*,[24] and *Minds That Came Back*.[25]**

---

*A series of documented descriptions of the open education system through detailed case examples is being published by the Citation Press: *Informal Schools in Britain Today*, 2 vols., 1972.

**There is a quite extensive literature on potentiality development which runs the compass from such balanced volumes as Gardner Murphy's,[26] John W. Gardner's,[27, 28] and Gordon Allport's,[29] to some of the more extreme items in Herbert A. Otto's collections.[30–32] This literature could be the subject of considerable critical study and evaluation.

From a program which deals with the latent resources of man, as well as with the obstacles and handicaps standing in the way of his use of them, from a program which deals in rounded fashion with man's personality, recognizing his cognitive capacities as well as his "feelings," may evolve techniques that will at least lead to efforts to reduce the waste in human resources so challenging to our culture today.[26–29, 30–32]

Educational Principles

Thus far we have been discussing the *substance* of what we should be teaching. But for teaching to be carried out in a concrete context, the particular pedagogic principles used to convey content most effectively are all-important.

Six major principles of context appear to me to be involved: (1) real-life settings to complement the more didactically represented aspects of the program; (2) establishment of general attitudes; (3) group participation in learning; (4) individualized techniques in learning; (5) unremitting environmental pressures; (6) and finally, and perhaps of greatest consequence, appropriate role models.

From the earliest days of the program and whenever possible thereafter, there should be emphasis on teaching concretely and in field situations—in *real-life settings*. Occasionally, simulated situations, as in some aspects of training in observation, are necessary; they at least have the advantage of being concrete. Also, whenever possible, the student himself should be an active participant. The emphasis should be on learning by doing rather than on learning by listening; there is little question which is the more effective. This is one way of deformalizing the educational process—an important principle for all education to follow whenever appropriate.

A primary attribute of the mental health worker is his recognition of the importance of *attitudes* in interpersonal relationships—both the patient's and his own. This is the sympathetic entry into the personal processes of another, as Gardner Murphy has put it.[33] The central place of attitudes is strengthened by an appeal from those in the position to benefit most: the patients. In *Beyond All Reason*, Morag Coate, who went through repeated episodes of schizophrenic psychosis and ultimately recovered, entitles a chapter "The Doctor's Role." This carries a fundamental message not unlike, though not as crass and literal, as the "Make love, not war" watchword of our young. Her theme is, "Like it or not, love is the guts of medicine."[34] (p. 206) She points out that "true love is not a comfortable, soft and sentimental feeling. . . . To care and let himself be cared about by his patients is an essential part of the doctor's role."[34] (pp. 206–7) This obviously holds as well for *all* workers in mental health.

Group participation, both within one's own profession and across professions, is one of the most effective learning devices we have. Cross-professional participation particularly deserves attention. How else capture the satisfactions which come from being part of a group striving toward a common social goal? There is a special satisfaction which springs from the eradication of the differences in status and background of the participants, making the work at hand—especially physical work, ordinarily considered menial in our culture—the conjoint project of all.

Two relatively recent endeavors (although there have been many such schemes, mainly utopian, in the past)—the Israeli kibbutz and the current Chinese Communist milieu—offer some constructive suggestions. The kibbutz made manual work primary and accorded it the highest status, whereas intellectual activity was given a decidedly secondary role. As Dan Jacobson has put it, "the best of life in a kibbutz was its physicality," and, I might add, the mutual conquest of difficulties. Though participation was a voluntary individual activity, it was to the utmost community-oriented. In fact, especially in its early days, the kibbutz was perhaps one of the most complete communistic societies ever developed—"selflessness" was the keystone of its social structure. In modern Mainland China, intellectual workers must spend part of their working time doing physical factory or farm work, so to gain a greater sense of identification with the factory or farm workers and to help abolish status differences. It is difficult to evaluate this practice adequately; though one hears increasing reports of its success, there are reports, too, of some of its failures. My major objection to it is its compulsory character, even if this compulsion is to a great extent based on community expectations.

The emphasis in both societies on the value and dignity of manual work, implying in this way the importance of the whole, rounded man and the breakdown of the boundaries between vocations, may contribute considerably to the realization of their social goals. If, parallel with this concentration on common group goals, we accord recognition to the importance of individuality and allow for basic personality differences, we would, I think, be on the way to achieving an "ideal" model for education.

I must emphasize further the importance of the student's *individuality* in the educational process. In my writings I have frequently referred to the Kluckhohn-Mowrer-Murray felicitous delineation of an individual's personality as comprising three kinds of characteristics, some like *all* other persons', some like *some other* persons', and some like *all* other persons'.[35 (pp. 53 ff.)] It is the last—the individual characteristics—rather than the universal and typical characteristics, that concern us in the present context. There are so many forces in our culture which, in their apparent efforts to reduce the complexities of a too complex life, work toward constricting both the limits of privacy and the importance of individuality. And in speaking of individuality, I am not, of course, referring to idiosyncrasy. In his discussion of the meaning of evolution, Simpson indicates, from a biologist's viewpoint, how important for this process is the maintenance of man's evolved individuality.[36] If we are to save the best aspects of our civilization, must we not labor ceaselessly to foster nature's gift of individual differences?

The problem revolves in part around the continuing development in the professional trainee of the responsibility and resourcefulness which should have been begun in early childhood. Settings should be designed in which the student becomes involved and develops a sense of responsibility toward the patient, the student himself carrying as much of the burden as is feasible. That cardinal pedagogical principle of stretching the student just a little beyond his capacity is a good guide. Most teachers tend to underestimate their students, and consequently fail to take advantage of their potentialities. An atmosphere of warm concern for the client should, of course, characterize the setting, yet the student must have an opportunity to make errors and to correct them. This universal educational paradox of the helping professions can be partly reconciled by providing the student with situations carrying the least hazards for the patient.

Since teaching is itself an effective mode of learning, opportunities for the student to teach should be multiplied. In the earlier years of the training program, teaching nurses, assistants, and technicians, and in the later years, teaching students of less advanced status, offer obvious possibilities.

Although the student might, under certain circumstances, be placed entirely on his own, he should ordinarily work with the degree of preceptorial guidance appropriate to his stage of development. The preceptor's personality and judgment, of course, play an important role in this process of building up independence. A certain degree of neglect is implicit in such a process, but that neglect should be studied and deliberate and aimed at promoting resourcefulness and individuality.

Unremitting *environmental pressures* are another necessary part of the educational program. I have, in discussing the problem of individual development, emphasized the need for stretching the individual. But this need must be broadened to include the whole program, since it works in groups as well as in individuals. Its relationship to the Jamesian tenet of tapping the energies of men is obvious.

The last of our contextual principles is the part played by *role models*. Perhaps the most important factor for developing the kinds of workers we hope for lies in the caliber of the exemplars—the teachers we provide. Unfortunately, relatively few of our teachers provide role models worthy of emulation. Thus, in a study by Gordon Allport of 100 students, mostly sophomores and juniors, he found that of the 4,600 or so teachers these students had had during their educational careers, only about 8.5 percent had had a "very strong or powerful influence" on the students' intellectual or personal development.[29] (pp. 171–83) Models seem crucial also for the ethical principles students adopt, the humility they develop in the face of the complex problems they have to deal with, and the freedom they achieve from too much dependence on orthodoxy.

With an emphasis upon courses, there is a tendency to pay less attention to the vehicles through which these courses are taught. In the end, it is surprising how much more permanent an impact teachers have on students by what they *do* in the context of what they say, rather than by what they merely say. And the impact is even greater when they also make it possible for the student himself to do the doing. Professors, who *do* in both these ways can contribute significantly toward realizing our aims. In this process, the influence communicated by nonverbal techniques is striking. I might, in passing, also point to the great advantage of using senior professors to teach first-year students.

Given the breadth of the mental health field, and its representation in the biological as well as the social and behavioral sciences, the range of potential model-serving exemplars is indeed wide. Ordinarily one does not find a single teacher who represents an amalgam of all the qualities to be emulated; more frequently the student, largely implicitly, constructs from aspects selected from several teachers a composite ideal which he integrates with his own individuality, and thus perhaps more easily creates for himself a model of a broadly based, humanized mental health worker.

Models, as I have already hinted, play the primary role in conveying ethical principles. On a number of occasions, when discussing problems of education in the "helping professions," I have found myself falling back on Felix Frankfurter's description of his training at the Harvard Law School:

> There weren't any courses on ethics, but the place was permeated by ethical presuppositions and assumptions and standards. On the whole, to this day I am rather leery of explicit ethical

instruction. It is something that you ought to breathe in. It was the quality of the feeling that dominated the place largely because of the dean, James Barr Ames. We had no course in ethics, but this course on law of trusts and fiduciary relations was so much more compelling as a course in ethics than any formal course in ethics that I think ill of most courses in ethics.[37] (p. 19)

Thinking of this theme, I recall an excerpt from a letter written over a century and a quarter ago. Thoreau had just visited Henry James, Sr., and afterwards, in writing to Emerson, said, "It makes humanity seem more erect and respectable. . . . I know of no one so patient and determined to have the good of you."[38] (p. 19) What better way to close a discussion of role models—this most important of the six educational principles involved in the training of human beings who are to invest their professional lives in trying to help other human beings? It is in the context of all these principles that I see carried out a substantive program like that I have outlined, and, I believe, under conditions which would have considerable likelihood for success.

Aside from leaving to each group the decision regarding the selection of what it considers the best training centers for its own purposes, it would be relevant to indicate some general principles of choice of setting for all those being trained to carry on research in mental health. These settings conveniently fall into three types: nonprofessional, educational, and professional. Among nonprofessional settings we might include those of field, factory, and community, the institutions where most of our daily, ordinary, nonfamilial activities take place. The educational settings include school environments of all kinds. The professional settings include those institutions and community settings which are directly concerned with treating the physically handicapped and mentally aberrant. In all three types of settings, the student's participation may occur during his preprofessional period—say, during high school or college—or be experienced later, when it is definitely a part of his professional training.

The nonprofessional settings offer a rich source of experience for contact with varieties of human nature—particularly with those represented in different age groups, different ethnic groups, and different socioeconomic levels—in fact, with all the class memberships that so frequently mask underlying differences among individuals. Whether it be experience with scout, club, camp, or church activities, whether it be experience in factory, store, office, labor union, or community organization—all such settings afford opportunities to observe and interact with a wide diversity of persons and to play a useful role in building up the apperceptive mass of knowledge about normal people that provides so important a baseline for understanding the disordered. The nonprofessional setting offers opportunities as well, though much less frequently, for observations at the more extreme ends of the behavioral scale—the benign as well as the malign.

School settings of all kinds are, of course, the dominant ones in the educational area, although some attention should also be paid to opportunities for participation in such educational institutions as museums and libraries. From nursery school through college there is an unparalleled opportunity to observe the range of normal development—again, experience which has inestimable value for a balanced appreciation of divergencies in development. Too few persons in the mental health field have had adequate experience with normal development, especially at the nursery school and Headstart level, where much of the groundwork for later behavior is laid.

The professional settings include all those institutions provided by our society to take care of the physically and mentally handicapped—hospitals and clinics, institutions for the delinquent, for the physically disabled, for the aged, etc., etc. In occasional instances, some experiences will, because of spontaneous interest, have been acquired by the student even before his formal involvement in mental health training. If this has not occurred, however, he should be encouraged to spend holiday and other free time in such institutions. An excellent example of this practice is the experiments engaging college students as attendants in state hospitals during the summer, or even in free time during the college year.

But more important is the judicious employment of "poor" institutions as a supplemental training ground for students from the superior institutions, where they have such advantages as good supervision and multidisciplinary representation. These "poor" environments, where treatment is much less intensive and where, because of understaffing, little or no supervision can be provided, offer resourceful students, at certain stages of their careers, ideal opportunities for testing out procedures that are ordinarily not possible in adequately supervised institutions. I have observed the blindness of many students (and some supervisors, as well) to the opportunities afforded in such settings—settings which unfortunately surround us on all sides but which offer them so much occasion for growth.

Conclusions

What would one expect to come out of a program such as I have outlined? My answer, I suppose, would be something like this:

First, I would expect that it would give rise to a wide range of persons, from the most intensely trained to the least trained—all directed at making some particular contribution to mental health. I am sure there would also be as wide a range in the degree of their involvement in research. A few would become full-time basic researchers, some full-time applied researchers, some part-time researchers, and some no-time researchers.

Second, my hope would be that a very considerable number of those who had undergone the training would come out with the questioning attitude the field so badly needs, and arrive at a position of being both more appreciative of, as well as more critical of, the research being done.

Third, I am myself impressed with how near I have come to proposing a kind of scientist-professional model, a model which I have for so long advocated in training for clinical psychology. At the present stage of progress in the field of mental health, this close combination of training, in both research and professional activity, with as much integration between didactic and field training as can possibly be achieved, still seems to me the goal of choice.

Fourth, I believe the program would encourage more initiative and experimentation, whatever the setting, in testing out novel techniques, the use of new personnel, etc. For example, I would expect greater use of patients as auxiliary personnel (with therapeutic gains for themselves), recruitment of new groups of students and workers, and new forms of therapies and institutional settings.

Fifth, I would expect more open and better relationships among the personnel involved, with greater appreciation of the range of the field and for each other's importance, contributions, and potential contributions.

Sixth, I would expect some reduction in the manpower shortage, since I believe that the program would, because of its philosophy, not only attract and enlist more personnel but, because of the emphasis on tapping their potentialities, would lead to some increased contribution from many of the individuals already participating in the program.

I am not suggesting that the program I have proposed would provide the panacea for all our ills. But I do think it would move us forward considerably—for one, in giving research its proper place in the field of mental health, and for another, in making available a greater use of people at closer to their full potential; but above all, in training researchers who will deal with *the* crucial problem of all education: to determine the best ways to develop persons who are inner-directed and self-starting, persons who will not only accept what the environment offers in the way of education, but who will, with *commitment*, set their own course.

NOTES

1. W. James, *Memories and Studies* (New York: Longmans, Green & Co., 1911).

2. W. James, "The Energies of Men," *Science* 25:321–32, 1907.

3. N.S. Shaler, *The Autobiography of Nathaniel Southgate Shaler, with a Memoir by His Wife* (Boston: Houghton Mifflin Co., 1909).

4. D. Shakow, "Psychopathology and Psychology—A Note on Trends." Published in Spanish: "Psicopatologia y Psicologia—Nota Sobre Tendencias," *Revista de Psicologia General y Aplicada* (Madrid) 15:835–37, 1960.

5. W. James, *Varieties of Religious Experience: A Study in Human Nature* (New York: Longmans, Green & Co., 1902.

6. D. Cooper, Introduction to *Madness and Civilization*, by M. Foucault (London: Tavistock Publications, 1967).

7. L. Trilling, *Sincerity and Authenticity* (Cambridge: Harvard University Press, 1972).

8. P.D. MacLean, "The Triune Brain, Emotion, and Scientific Bias," in *The Neurosciences: Second Study Program*, ed. F. O. Schmitt (New York: Rockefeller University Press, 1970).

9. R.F. Scott, *Scott's Last Expedition* (London: Smith Elder & Co., 1913).

10. A. Cherry-Garrard, *The Worst Journey in the World*, 2 vol. (London: Penguin Books, 1937).

11. M. Sechehaye, *Autobiography of a Schizophrenic Girl* (New York: Signet Books, 1970).

12. M. Milner, *The Hands of the Living God: An Account of a Psychoanalytic Treatment* (New York: International Universities Press, 1969).

13. R. D'Ambrosio, *No Language But a Cry* (Garden City, N.Y.: Doubleday & Co., 1970).

14. W.M. Axline, *Dibs: In Search of Self* (New York: Ballantine Books, 1971).

15. N. Hunt, *The World of Nigel Hunt: The Diary of a Mongoloid Youth* (Beaconsfield, Eng., Darwen Finlayson, 1967).

16. H. Keller, *The Story of My Life* (New York: Doubleday, Page & Co., 1903).

17. "Peggy," N. Cousins, *Saturday Review*, September 11, 1971, pp. 28–29.

18. B. Bettelheim, "Individual and Mass Behavior in Extreme Situations," *J Abnorm Soc Psychol* 38:417–52, 1943.

19. V.E. Frankl, *From Death-Camp to Existentialism* (Boston: Beacon Press, 1959).

20. N.E. Miller, L.V. DiCara, H. Solomon, J.M. Weiss, and B. Dworkin, "Learned Modifications of Autonomic Functions: A Review and Some New Data," in *Biofeedback and Self-Control: An Aldine Annual on the Regulation of Bodily Processes and Consciousness*, ed. T. X. Barber et al. (Chicago: Aldine-Atherton, 1971).

21. J. Featherstone, *Schools Where Children Learn* (New York: Liveright, 1971).

22. J. Featherstone, "Open Schools. I. The British and Us. II. Tempering a Fad," *New Republic*, September 11, 1971, pp. 20–25; September 25, 1971, pp. 17–21.

23. J.D. Adams, ed., *Triumph Over Odds: An Anthology of Man's Unconquerable Spirit* (New York: Duel, Sloan & Pearce, 1957).

24. A. Boisen, *Out of the Depths* (New York: Harper & Brothers, 1960).

25. W.C. Alvarez, *Minds That Came Back* (Philadelphia: J.B. Lippincott Co., 1961).

26. G. Murphy, *Human Potentialities* (New York: Basic Books, 1958).

27. J.W. Gardner, *Excellence* (New York: Harper & Row, 1962).

28. J.W. Gardner, *Self-Renewal* (New York: Harper & Row, 1965).

29. G. Allport, *The Person in Psychology: Selected Essays* (Boston: Beacon Press, 1968).

30. H.A. Otto, ed., *Explorations in Human Potentialities* (Springfield, Ill: Charles C. Thomas, 1966).

31. H.A. Otto, ed., *Human Potentialities: The Challenge and the Promise* (St Louis: Warren H. Green, 1968).

32. H.A. Otto, ed., *Ways of Growth: Approaches to Expanding Awareness* (New York: Viking Press, 1968).

33. G. Murphy, *Freeing Intelligence Through Teaching* (New York: Harper & Brothers, 1961).

34. M. Coate, *Beyond All Reason* (Philadelphia: J.B. Lippincott. Co., 1965).

35. C. Kluckhohn and H.A. Murray, eds., *Personality in Nature, Society, and Culture* (New York: Alfred A. Knopf, 1953).

36. G.G. Simpson, *The Meaning of Evolution* (New Haven: Yale University Press, 1949).

37. F. Frankfurter, *Felix Frankfurter Reminisces* (Garden City, N.Y.: Doubleday & Co., 1962).

38. F.B. Sanborn, ed., *Familiar Letters of Henry David Thoreau* (Boston: Houghton Mifflin Co., 1894).

AN ASHENDENE DOZEN FROM THE LEVI A. OLAN COLLECTION OF FINE BOOKS

DECHERD TURNER

ON March 22, 1963, a cross-section of Dr. Levi Olan's many friends from North Texas provided as their expression of regard on the occasion of his birthday the funds for the establishment of The Levi A. Olan Collection of Fine Books.

Since that time, additional gifts have been made for supporting the collection so that it has continued to grow. The collection now numbers approximately fifteen hundred volumes, and it is housed in the Special Collections areas of Bridwell Library, Southern Methodist University, Dallas, Texas.

The major contours of the collection give definition to the book as an art object in its own right—design and production, and continuing condition.

As a natural part of the growth pattern, certain areas have emerged with strength in numbers and depth. And it was almost predestined (if one can use such a word regarding anything connected with Rabbi Olan, as well as a Methodist institution) bibliographically that one of the interests in which Dr. Olan and Bridwell Library would find great harmony of interest and purpose was in the publications of the Ashendene Press.

The work of the Ashendene Press (1895–1935), along with the Kelmscott Press (1891–1896) and the Doves Press (1900–1917), formed the basis for the revival of printing which made the twentieth century typographically the most interesting century since the last fifty years of the fifteenth century (which was the first fifty years of printing: 1450–1500). For it was the delibreate purpose of these three presses to recapture the very best of the bookmaking arts which Eden-like had flourished most brilliantly at the beginning of the typographic era. William Morris of the Kelmscott took the lead in his insistence on the best of materials (handmade paper, the appropriate font of type, and black ink), craftsmanship (only by the usage of the hand press could the highest quality of printing be obtained), and taste (that combination of materials and craftsmanship which gives the most visible theological expression, since taste is a gift of God).

The standards set by the productions of these three presses have formed the corpus of quality to which all book people repair for refreshment in a bibliographic atmosphere in which there is no compromise with less than the best. It will soon be a century now (the first Kelmscott Press book came out in 1891) since the beginning of this important movement; and if by some dramatic and terrible event all fifteenth-century printing were destroyed, bibliographic archaeology could reconstruct from the Kelmscott-Doves-Ashendene books the first canons and principles of fine bookmaking.

Between the three founding-father presses of the twentieth-century revival there are differences of emphasis, however. Otherwise, what a boring repetition of perfection! And it is at this precise point that the Ashendene Press forms a type of middle ground, utilizing the best and most distinctive qualities of both the Kelmscott and the Doves. In other words, it is the most "reasoned" press of the three. While an Ashendene Press book occasionally sports an introductory page border, such does not overwhelm the text as Kelmscott borders are wont to do. On the other hand, the usage of woodcut initials and two specially designed typefaces, after having early in its career used Fell and Caslon, gives the Ashendene books a far greater variety than was ever possible with the spartan devotion of Doves to one font of type. And, in the choice of texts to print, no more wonderful sentence has been written by a printer about his work than "My choice has therefore fallen in the majority of cases upon books which gave scope for a certain gaity of treatment in the use of coloured initials and chapter-headings . . . ''

And there is the matter of time. Forty books in forty years! Plus a number of important ephemeral pieces. The relatively short-lived brilliance of the Kelmscott and Doves Presses gives way to the seasoned, deliberate production of the Ashendene, which shows greater bibliographic grace with each item published.

To those who have worked with Rabbi Olan (this is the twenty-fifth year of our colleagueship), there will be no further need to expound the "inevitability" of the development of an Ashendene Collection within the confines of the larger Olan Collection.

One dozen Ashendene volumes have been chosen for bibliographic profile. It has been natural in collecting Ashendenes that interest would be stronger in the more mature years of the press's work, and that is reflected in the choice here. It was felt appropriate to choose eleven books of the forty printed—and one ephemeral piece, Mr. Hornby called them "minor pieces," (the last from the press) for profile.

Eighteenth Book

BIBLE. *A Book of Songs and Poems from the Old Testament and the Apocrypha.* 1904.

In the magnificent-folio period of the Ashendene Press, still about three decades off, there was to be great grandeur, great dignity; and in order to support such qualities, the book itself became big and iconographic.

At this point of the Ashendene Press, we are within the time range of the smaller, more intimate volume, and this chaste little selection forms one of the most attractive books of the Ashendene corpus.

Printed on Batchelor handmade paper with hammer and anvil watermark, with headings printed in red, and the hand-supplied blue initials by Graily Hewitt—all combine in great harmony to make a superbly pleasant volume.

One hundred fifty copies were printed on paper, of which this is one. Twenty-five copies were printed on vellum. A number of the vellum copies were especially decorated by Miss Florence Kingsford (Mrs. Sydney Cockerell). Bound in vellum. Printer's device A was cut on wood by Edward Whymper, and is a representation of the printing press from sixteenth-century drawing by Jost Amman.

Twenty-second Book

SIR THOMAS MORE. *Utopia*. 1906.

This is the first Ashendene volume with most of the shoulder notes printed in red, and what a stunning addition it makes. With the chapter and paragraph initials designed by Eric Gill, all done in red, the whole result makes a serious argument that the Ashendene books are much more attractive when in red and black than when additional colors are used in chapter or paragraph initials—as in the *Ecclesiasticus*.

One hundred copies were printed on Batchelor paper with bugle watermark, of which this is one. Twenty copies were printed on vellum.

Bound in blue boards with linen back. The volume does not bear a printer's device.

Twenty-sixth Book

SIR THOMAS MALORY. *Le Morte Darthur*. 1913.

This is the first appearance of the blue used alternately with the red to print the chapter initials so superbly designed by Graily Hewitt. And it is a blue which in the printing, with the exception of the *Decameron* (to appear in 1920), somehow does not fit. Where the reds and the blacks stand on the paper, the blue lie on the paper. It's just the difference between vitality and languor. Nevertheless, this volume stands with the superior company of magnificent books of any age. It is simply impossible to conceive of a time when the Ashendene *Morte Darthur* wouldn't command special attention.

Woodcuts by C. M. and Margaret Gere, two of them full-page, evoke the proper Camelot-sad mood.

One hundred and forty-five copies were printed on paper, of which this is one. Eight copies were printed on vellum. The present copy is bound in brown calf.

Twenty-ninth Book

BOCCACCIO. *Decameron*. 1920.

On those opening pages where the headings of the Giornata printed in blue combine with the headings of the Novella printed in red, the results are wonderfully satisfying. And yet how different a page in the same book appears when one turns to a page of text which has no color aside from one single shoulder-note printed in red. Here the dignity of Subiaco type shows forth in all its magisterial glory.

One hundred and five copies were printed on Batchelor with the bugle watermark, of which this is one. There are also six copies on vellum. This copy is bound in blue boards with linen back and printed label on spine. Printing was started on this volume in 1913. Before it was half-finished the work was interrupted by World War I, and the rest of the printing was not finished until 1920.

In his bibliography, St John Hornby recounts an amazing event concerning one copy of this edition:

In 1927 an amusing incident occurred in connection with this book. A copy sent by Messrs. Maggs, the London booksellers, to a client in the State of Kansas, U.S.A., was impounded by the Post

Office authorities of the United States and, in spite of protests, destroyed as an "immoral book"! I myself saw the mutilated copy returned to Messrs. Maggs as "evidence of destruction." This banning and wanton destruction of a great classic in the original language seems to be worth recording as somewhat of a curiosity in the annals of censorship. I understand that the U. S. Customs Bureau have since relented and that certain editions of the Decameron may now be imported into the United States.

Thirty-first Book

FRANCIS OF ASSISI. *I Fioretti del Glorioso Poverello di Christo S. Francesco di Assisi.* 1922.

The Italian text is carried out in the colophon, and somehow Chelsea and its location never sounded quite as grand: " . . . Impresso nell' amena città di Chelsea sulla riva del Tamigi per opera e spese di StJohn Hornby nella sua Officina Privata di Ashendene . . . "

Printed on Batchelor paper with watermark of anvil and hammer; shoulder-notes and chapter-headings are printed in red, and opening initial of each chapter printed in red or blue from design by Graily Hewitt. The woodcut illustrations were drawn by Charles M. Gere, and cut on wood by J. B. Swain.

It takes a strong dosage of temerity to criticize any Ashendene book, and in particular the color of an initial designed by Graily Hewitt. However, Texans having an excess of that commodity, it does appear that the tint of blue used in initial letters is slightly off. More aqua than blue, such color just does not appear in harmony with the blackness of the black, and the redness of the red.

Two hundred and forty copies were printed on paper, of which this is one. Twelve copies were printed on vellum. Issued in the usual binding style of "revival of fine printing"—vellum with green ties!

With printer's device C, designed by Philip Webb.

Thirty-second Book

EDMUND SPENSER. *The Faerie Queene*. 1923.

The largest book produced by the Ashendene Press, and a tremendously handsome production it is. Monumentality is obtained—and yet in spite of the size and awesome dignity of Subiaco type in two columns per page—there are qualities of approachableness which are difficult to obtain in a folio of this proportion. It is kind of like suggesting something more intimate to a famous statue—chances are against it, but the inclination is there nevertheless.

The beginning initials designed by Graily Hewitt and printed alternately in blue and red are attractive in their design, although, as will be noted, in annotations of Ashendene books where the blue is printed, particularly the initials alone, there are serious questions as to the relationship of the tone of the blue to the tones of the black and red.

One hundred and eighty copies were printed on paper, of which this is one, bound in ivory vellum sides with brown cowhide back. Also twelve copies on vellum were printed. Printer's device D, printed in red.

Following the colophon, realizing that a folio of this size evokes the most demonic tendencies of binders to trim with their knives, the printer addresses this plea:

An humble Prayer of the Printer to future Binders of this volume. The Printer having sorrowfully noted the wanton & irreparable damage done to many fine books at the hands of the Binders of past ages by the cropping of their edges and the consequent spoiling of the fair proportions of their margins, humbly prays the Binders of the future into whose hands copies of this book may fall to spare the knife and leave the edges, as he hopes they may find them unmutilated. And so may the blessing of God rest upon them & prosper them in their handiwork.

Thirty-sixth Book

CERVANTES. *Don Quixote, translated out of the Spanish by Thomas Shelton*. 1927–28.

Almost three years in printing, *Don Quixote* never had more excellent dress. The two folio volumes, the first printed in the Ashendene Ptolemy type, set in double columns, fill with tasteful precision all the canons of fine bookmaking. In many ways, the volumes form a whole anthology of bibliographic masterpieces: the borders remind one of the great Venetian white-vine borders, and more nearly contemporaneously, the borders of William Morris; the woodcut initials are wonderfully reminiscent of the great incunable printer Erhard Ratdolt; the combination of black and red suggest a Doves-type page.

Initials and borders were designed by Louise Powell. There were 225 copies on paper, and the Olan copy is bound in morocco. An additional twenty copies were printed on vellum. Printer's device D is printed in red.

Thirty-seventh Book

THUCYDIDES. *Thucydides, translated into English by Benjamin Jowett*. 1930.

One of the noble folios from the Ashendene Press, and it is a nobility of such strength and merit that only the finer volumes of the incunable period and the Kelmscott *Chaucer* can compare.

The colophon notes that it took almost two years for the presswork. Printed in Ptolemy type, particularly pleasant for massive folios. The first line of each book was designed by Graily Hewitt and is printed in red. Shoulder-notes are in red, Blado Italic, and bring a warmth that is badly needed for pages of such dimensions. Mr. Hewitt also designed three-line chapter initials, which are printed in red.

Paper copies numbered 260, and were bound in white pigskin. The Olan copy is one of these. Twenty copies were also printed on vellum.

Printer's device D appears on the verso of the last page, and makes a striking appearance in black, standing alone on the great white page.

Thirty-eighth Book

ECCLESIASTICUS. *The Wisdom of Jesus, the Son of Sirach, commonly called Ecclesiasticus.* 1932.

One of the most praised of the Ashendene volumes. While the Subiaco type makes a stunning black impression on the page, and the shoulder-notes and chapter-headings printed in red provide colorful contrast, the chapter and initial letters in blue and green, done by hand by Graily Hewitt and his associates, leave one with some sense of incompatibility. The green, in particular, is like a sour note in an otherwise perfect symphony.

St. John Hornby in his summary of the work of his press notes the circumstances of the usage of this text:

> The printing of this book was due to the fact that my friend and partner, A. D. Power, had with the help of one or two Hebrew scholars compiled from the various versions of "Ecclesiasticus" a text which he subsequently caused to be written out on vellum and illuminated by A. J. Fairbank and Louise Powell respectively in a volume of great beauty. One day he happened to tell me that he thought of having the version printed, as many of his friends wished to possess it. The temptation to add yet one more book to my list was too strong for me to resist and I here and then offered to print a small edition. I have never regretted having done so, as in my humble judgment it is one of the most satisfying of the books of the Press.

Three hundred and twenty-eight copies were printed on Batchelor paper with the bugle watermark, of which this is one. Twenty-five copies were printed on vellum. The paper copies were bound in orange vellum with silk ties. With printer's device D, designed in the office of Emery Walker. Olan copy in slipcase.

Thirty-ninth Book

LONGUS. *Les Amours Pastorales de Daphnis et Chloe. Traduction de Messire J. Amyot.* 1933.

This is one of the most beautiful books of the twentieth century. Perhaps the striking difference is that the Olan copy is one printed on vellum (290 had been printed on paper, and 20 on vellum). There is a brilliance of color which is supported by the vellum background which cannot be created with any other materials.

Initials and paragraph marks are filled in by hand in blue, with the chapter initials laid on in gold, by Graily Hewitt and his associates. Gwendolen Raverat designed and cut the woodcuts. When one turns the book to the opening of the chapters, the combination of the black of the woodcut and type, the simple gold lines of the opening letter, the red of the shoulder-notes and the chapter heading, and perhaps the blue of a paragraph mark—what more in bibliographic splendor can be asked? Where else can it be found making its statement in such restrained, and yet fulfilled, elegance?

This printing of *Daphnis et Chloe* by the Ashendene Press is the result of a disappointing accident concerning the first printing. The printing was completed in 1931. Mr. StJohn Hornby describes the events that followed thus:

> Unfortunately the ink used was very slow in drying and the sheets were packed before it had sufficiently hardened. The mistake was not discovered until the sheets were unpacked at the binders when it was found that very bad "set-off" had occurred on many of them. As the book would have been unworthy of the Press I reluctantly decided to destroy the whole edition with the exception of 10 copies, which I had made up from the least spoiled sheets, and some odd specimen pages. . . . They are not to be considered perfect, nor do they rank as one of the regular issues of the Ashendene Press, having been preserved as specimens only.

Bound in green morocco, in slip case. Printer's device A appears on title page, and device C at the end.

Fortieth Book

ASHENDENE PRESS. *A Descriptive Bibliography of the Books Printed at The Ashendene Press MDCCCXCV–MCMXXXV.* Chelsea, Shelley House, 1935.

The catalogue raisonné of the Ashendene Press is one of the most complete and beautiful ever prepared. It profiles a tremendous legacy to the book world, and that world has responded appropriately by its willingness to match its quality with dollars for purchase.

Sample pages of the volumes produced, combined with bibliographical detail and a graceful foreword by StJohn Hornby, along with information on ephemera produced by the press—all are facets which make for high usability, as well as comfort and pleasure of the eye.

The first line of the colophon is worth repeating: "This book, the last from the Ashendene Press, was printed at Shelley House, Chelsea, by C. H. StJ. Hornby with the help of A. J. Fisk, compositor, and H. Gage-Cole, pressman, and was finished in the month of February, 1935, forty years after the date of the first book printed at the Press . . . "

No. 268 of 390 copies, signed by Mr. StJohn Hornby. Bound in calf with the outlines of printer's device D tooled in gold on front. In slipcase.

Minor Pieces (the last)

ASHENDENE PRESS. *A Chronological list, with prices of the forty books printed at The Ashendene Press MDCCCXCV–MCMXXXV.* Chelsea, Shelley House, 1935.

Four leaves sewn in printed wrapper, with printer's device B1 on cover.

A very special aura surrounds this folio booklet. The final page of text bears this statement: "This final list of the books of the Ashendene Press was printed for private circulation only in the month of March, 1935."

It is indeed a final list. But there is no finality in the influence and sheer bibliographic joy and instruction that others have taken from this inexhaustible source.

****

And so we have raised a bibliographic standard in salute to Dr. Olan. Just why the Ashendene Press was chosen should be clear by now. The parallels are too obvious for further elaboration.

A PRELIMINARY SUMMING UP

LEVI A. OLAN

THE contributors of this volume are scholars and friends. The diversity of their intellectual disciplines has helped to expand my interests and to arouse my envy of their talents. I regret the opportunities carelessly neglected for comradely visits with them. Each has helped shape my thinking and deserves my gratitude. The publication of this volume by Congregation Emanu-El to mark my achieving the first part of the biblical "days of our years" is one of many generous and kindly deeds with which they have blessed me during the past quarter of a century. It is very good to offer thanks for these blessings.

A review of my writings and lectures during the almost half century in which they occurred discloses the intriguing statistic that my most common title was "The Faith of an Untired Liberal." During these five decades, liberals had experienced frustration and a failure of nerve. Their shining hopes were shattered by a devastating depression, by the rise of Nazism and Fascism, and by Hiroshima with its promise of the nuclear annihilation of a large portion of the world's population. At each nadir I reaffirmed my faith in liberalism. In the face of the present mood of despair and the aggravated human condition, the old title recently gave way to "It Is Later Than You Think."

History, in the language of the Bible, alternates between the prophetic and the apocalyptic. In the first, man can save himself from disaster by doing justly, loving mercy, and walking humbly. In the second, salvation is the work of a supernatural power which acts for reasons of its own. The exile of Israel in 586 B.C.E. affords a suitable illustration in history when men were confronted with a choice between these two alternatives. They had been brought to Babylon by their captors to live as aliens and prisoners. Their faith in Yahweh was shaken, He had let them down. Hopelessness and despair overwhelmed them. What or who would save them now?

One answer had popular appeal. Ezekiel assured the forlorn exiles that even though their unjust and immoral behavior did not deserve it, God would save them *L'ma'an Shemo*, for His own sake, to fulfill His own purpose in history. "For I will take you from among nations and gather you out of all the countries and will bring you to your own land. . . . a new heart will I also give you and a new spirit will I put within you . . . and I will call for the corn and increase it, and lay no famine upon you. And I will multiply the fruit of the tree and the increase of the field. . . . not for your sake will I do this, saith the Lord God." This is salvation by faith. God, because He is God, ultimately saves His people. In an earlier age such salvation was called *Yom Yahweh*, The Day of the Lord. It was the "great come-and-get-it-day." All that was asked of the people was faithful performance of the sacred rites—animal sacrifices, prescribed libations, and tithing to provide for the Temple service. So long as they meet these ecclesiastical requirements, God will deliver them from the worst of catastrophes because, to paraphrase Heine, that is His business. This is the apocalyptic view of history.

There was another answer and it was not popular at all. It began with the assertion that the cruel disaster they were suffering was the result of their failure to abide by the moral covenant under which they lived. The "day of the Lord" was not the day of salvation, but the day of judgment. It will not be the end of the exile and the beginning of peace and prosperity. The nation's tragic calamity was brought about by the moral failure of the people. Salvation was not only God's business, it was also dependent upon a radical transformation of the moral values by which the people lived. Jeremiah prophesied in the same dark period of Jewish history as did Ezekiel. He saw the people throng the Temple with their animal offerings as they reverently worshipped God. There was little question in their minds that the threatening destruction by the Babylonians would be averted. But the prophet stood in the Temple court and warned the people against the comfortable faith that God would rescue them in their hour of doom. "Nay, but if ye thoroughly amend your ways and your doings; if ye thoroughly execute justice between a man and his neighbor; if ye oppress not the stranger, the fatherless, and the widow, and shed not innocent blood in this place; . . . then I will cause you to dwell in this place, in the land that I gave to your fathers, forever and ever." This is the prophetic view of history.

There is little doubt that the apocalyptic view of history has the greater popular appeal when disaster looms ahead. Ezekiel is a more acceptable leader in time of crisis than Jeremiah. When the situation is desperate, even hopeless, only God or a miracle can save it. The appeal to a radical change in the people's way of life, to do good and not evil as a road to salvation in an hour of despair, is like meeting the Babylonian armies with a water pistol. What is needed is a miracle.

The apocalyptic became the dominant philosophy of history in the Western world. A messiah, in a variety of forms, was eagerly expected to redeem the world from its agony. Jews chanted "next year in Jerusalem" as the time when God will bring peace and plenty to all mankind and Israel will return to the land of Abraham, Isaac, and Jacob. Some false messiahs, Shabbatai Zevi and Jacob Frank, cynically raised vain hopes in the breasts of thousands of Jews in the seventeenth and eighteenth centuries. Christianity, the predominant faith and culture of Europe, lived with the hope of the Second Coming of Christ and the salvation of all believers. God, through grace, will transport men from a world of corruption and suffering to a life of blessing and joy. Until the modern era Ezekiel and Paul, the apocalyptic voices of an earlier day, molded and encouraged the hopes of the age of faith.

The prophetic view of history was revived by the Enlightenment and its by-product, the Emancipation. The agents of human redemption in this new era were reason and science. Heinrich Heine, over a century ago, speaking of the rebellious young writers in Germany, wrote: "A new faith inspires them with a passion. . . . This is a faith in progress, a faith which springs from science. We have measured the earth, weighed the forces of nature, calculated the resources of industry, and behold—we have found that the earth is spacious and wide, enough for everyone to build his hut of happiness upon it; that the earth can feed us all decently if only each of us works, and none lives at another's expense; that it is no longer necessary to preach the blessedness of heaven to the masses of the poor." The advocates of this shining hope became known as liberals, those aimed at liberating mankind from the oppressive chains that bound it mentally and physically to a wall of darkness and slavery.

Liberalism does not lend itself to a definition acceptable to everyone. For some, the term describes a society characterized by laissez-faire as practiced in nineteenth-century England and the United States. Today liberalism is defined by the social security programs already written into law and by measures which need to be enacted to provide adequate health care, job opportunity, old age pensions, and a host of currently proposed social legislation. These descriptions of liberalism which aim at a particular social or political platform are rejected by those who maintain that liberalism is an attitude of mind which favors freedom instead of authority. In this case it is a philosophy whose distinction is its rejection of a closed system of thought fenced in by fixed, unchanging dogma. Liberals of this kind take an intellectual approach to human problems, seeking ways to liberate man from all that enslaves him whether in mind or in society.

Liberalism as an attitude, or set of mind, is very old in human history. Ancient myths testify to its presence. The Gods became angry because men threatened to acquire more knowledge than was good for them. Prometheus was chained to a rock exposing him to a vulture who gnawed away at his liver. The crime for which Zeus punished him in this brutal manner was his theft of fire, symbol of reason and art. In the legend of the Tower of Babel, God is fearful lest men, possessing one language, will understand each other, and nothing will be able to stop them from what they purpose to do. He confounds their language and scatters them abroad. Adam and Eve are ejected from Paradise because they ate fruit from the forbidden tree of knowledge. They threatened to know what only God knows—good and evil. From the beginning, it appears, there existed a fear that intelligent men will learn more than they can, as human creatures, safely handle.

Historically, liberalism appears in Hebrew and Greek civilization questioning the validity of ancient beliefs and programs of salvation. In Israel the prophets challenged the popular religious dogma that faith without moral deeds will deliver men from destruction. They confronted men with a universe of law, physical and moral, and tried to persuade them that disobedience to the moral demands was as devastating as a violation of the law of nature. The day when men "will beat their swords into plowshares . . . every man shall sit under his vine and his fig tree; and none shall make them afraid" can be realized only if they do justly, love mercy, and walk humbly. The prophetic, like the liberalism of a later generation, placed the responsibility for redemption from disaster squarely upon man. There is a critical difference which cannot be ignored—the prophets required that men do what God requires. Modern liberalism, in the main, is secular in nature.

Socrates in the Hellenic world was a liberal. He died for the right to inquire freely and to express his thoughts without fear of authoritarian censorship. He taught that virtue derives from knowledge and from a continuing examination of one's beliefs. The unexamined life is not worth living. He, like the Hebrew Prophets, Job, and Ecclesiastes, represents in these ancient cultures the free inquiring mind in search of knowledge, the hallmark of liberalism. Descartes is considered the father of the Enlightenment. He introduced a new methodology of knowledge which constituted a radical break with the past. The door was opened for a critical examination of supernatural revelation as the source of truth. His appearance on the scene was not without precursive events. The Renaissance had reintroduced the rich secular culture of the past, directing men's interest away from the world beyond to this world. Protestantism promoted private judgment in the interpretation of the Bible, giving rise to individualism in religion. On the horizon there appeared diversity of sect instead of one authoritative church. Galileo and Newton had set in motion the scientific revolution of the seventeenth and eighteenth centuries. The world appeared to function like a machine run by universal laws, automatic and immutable, operating with infallible precision and with unfailing regularity. The scientific method became authoritative in man's understanding of nature, and reason the guide to knowledge of man and morals.

Two historic revolutions arose out of the intellectual ferment: the industrial, which challenged the feudal structure of the Middle Ages, and the French, which ushered in the democratic impulse in the Western world. When the nineteenth century dawned, the liberal outlook issued forth as a program for the liberation of man from all slavery—social, political, economic, and mental. Natural law now transformed the world from an enemy of man to a friend. A universe capable of being observed and measured can be manipulated to meet his needs. It follows, inevitably, that life must imitate nature. The acid test of any institution—economic, political, or social, is its degree of conformity to the law of nature. Institutions that work badly are dispensable and should be abolished. In human affairs, as well as in the realm of nature, the scientific method is authoritative.

Reason displaced faith as man's guide in his search for truth. The new intellectual mood defined man as a rational creature, though not always reasonable. He was endowed by nature or by God with a faculty to test all evidence for its rationality. Since reason was common to all men, it was seen as the uniting element in mankind which would lead to human brotherhood. Reason became the instrument man must use continually in his search after larger truths, acknowledging always that the truth he now declares is not an absolute. Somewhere there may exist one eternal and absolute truth, but the one we now know is not it. Man may have a natural Platonism, a world of universal ideas, which his knowledge only reflects. The world he now possesses is not perfection. To announce that he has hold of absolute truth is to attribute perfection to his own image. Man, a creature somewhat less than divine, must constantly use his mind to examine nature and himself in the hope that he may move a little closer to the truth.

Liberalism, which grew out of the Enlightenment, added another ingredient to support its faith in reason and science. It proclaimed that man is naturally good although he can be corrupted by ignorance and prejudice. Rousseau suggested that civilization spoiled him. To escape this destructive force he advocated a radical change in the social order, one more in harmony with man's natural goodness. Liberals were optimistic about the possibilities for the moral and intellectual development of mankind. They rejected the prevalent dogma that man is by nature a sinner and that his salvation lay in grace, not in himself. They believed that man is born ignorant, not wicked. His escape from the misery, pain, and suffering of the present hour depends upon a better use of his natural faculties, his mind, his conscious reason, and his innate goodness. The wise and prudent use of these will help him create an earthly utopia.

Belief in the possibility of progress became an inescapable and integral part of liberalism. Its basic premise is the conviction that man can move toward a better condition, that he may even point toward perfectability. In the nineteenth century this faith triggered a driving force. Things were happening to support this dynamic movement. The technological revolution introduced rapid changes which improved the conditions of life. There was greater wealth, larger cities, better means of transportation and communication, increasing security against disease and premature death, and a spectacular display of appliances to reduce the burden and drudgery of daily living. Progress was not a faith, it was a fact. There were those who were carried away with the shining prospects and, like Herbert Spencer, spoke of inevitable progress. Most liberals believed that man, by thinking wisely and acting vigorously, can make the world a better place in which to live. William James proposed the idea that progress makes life significant. ''That strange union of reality with ideal novelty . . . the solid meaning of life is always . . . the marriage of an unhabitual idea, however special, with some fidelity, courage, and endurance, with some man's or woman's pains.''

Darwin's theory exploded on the scene, and the idea of evolution enforced the liberal's faith in progress. The struggle for existence ended with the survival of the fittest. All of history, from the amoeba to Einstein, discloses a steady movement from the lower to the higher. The very nature of life itself validated the reality of progress. Karl Marx contributed to the liberal hope by introducing the dialectical materialism of history wherein class conflict leads inevitably to a classless utopia. As the twentieth century began, men were more certain than ever that the human race is growing better and becoming happier. There is no ceiling to its ultimate success. Lewis Morgan, an American anthropologist before the turn of the century, wrote: ''Democracy in government, brotherhood in society, equality in right and privilege, and universal education, foreshadow the next higher plane of society to which experience, intelligence, and knowledge are steadily tending.''

Somewhere, somehow, liberalism went wrong. Instead of bringing us utopia, it seems to have led us to a supreme crisis in history. Instead of normal change, where yesterday's way of life will give way to a new and better one in an orderly and regular pattern, we find ourselves violently torn loose from the world we knew and set adrift in an alien place. Change has become crisis, and men feel themselves on the verge of despair. Ours is a revolutionary age, not so much due to its violence, but because of the loss of confidence in rational man and his ability to overcome the unrelieved terror he experiences. The hope which the liberal had placed in the scientific method, in reason, in man's growth toward perfectability, and in progress ended up in the barbarism of Hitler and the madness of Stalin. Man discovered suddenly that he stood paralyzed before the very weapon his mind had fashioned. Was Zeus right? Our Prometheus did bring us to the brink of despair. Where did liberalism go wrong?

Its critics agree that the fallacy lies embedded in the very structure of the liberal philosophy. The categories which it applies to the study of history are too narrow and inadequate. Reason and science give a limited and even distorted view of the human experience. Reason is enslaved to unconscious wishes, to "the vague, veiled chaos of the human soul." Man's intellect has its limitations—a fact, its critics claim, the liberals neglected. Furthermore, liberals were deceived by the notion of human perfectability. The truth, it is now said, is that man is not only finite but is cursed with a desire to break the bounds of his human nature in order to attain the infinite. "To be a disappointed idealist is," as Reinhold Niebuhr wrote, "the common and eternal fate of all men." The paradox of the human situation is that man is doomed "to seek an impossible victory and adjust to an inevitable defeat." Liberalism, say its critics, did not go wrong. It was wrong from the beginning.

A variety of nostrums have been proposed to replace the discredited credentials of liberalism. They differ from ultimate skepticism to absolute dogma. They share in common a categorical rejection of the thesis that reason and science are reliable tools to improve the human condition. Man, they argue, must begin by recognizing his own helplessness and hopelessness. Some recommend that he make a leap from the natural absurdity of the human condition to salvation in the existential experience of the absolute. In a less radical vein he is urged to refurbish the old doctrine of eternal verities which are known only by faith. There is a rather large school of secular skeptics which denies that there is even the possibility for man to know what can help him in his despair. The revolt against the liberal faith brought together theologians, philosophers, social scientists, historians, and literary critics. They represent an intellectual revolution in search of a philosophy or a faith suitable to the human condition in the atomic age, a time of dreadful and total contingency of human existence.

Before the expiring body of liberalism is pronounced dead and the interment rites begin, it may be wise to arrange for a consultation and take another look at the diagnosis. The disasters of the past sixty years are real and grim. The notion that they are the consequences of a false optimism derived from a liberal philosophy is the product of hysteria rather than common sense. The disappointments modern man experiences arise in large part from the fact that he has come to expect more from life. People are unwilling to accept sickness, poverty, cruelty, ignorance, or war as permanent conditions. They are aware and impressed that men live longer, work is less burdensome, education is a possibility for everybody, and that leisure and enjoyment may be the lot of the many as well as the few. The violent revolutions of our age testify to rising expectations. There is more human concern for the welfare of the repressed and suffering peoples of the world today than ever before in history. Unlike the generations of the past, who were dumbly resigned to the fear and dread of starvation, disease, slavery, and the terrors of nature, the present generation knows that these evils need not exist. Man's discontents are loud testimony to his faith in the promises of liberalism.

The diagnosis which attributes the sickness of modern man to the infection produced by an overdose of liberalism is unsupported by legitimate evidence. What seems to be more to the point is that we have failed precisely in those areas of life where reason and science were not applied. It is clear that we hold in our hands the capacity to produce enough basic goods to wipe out poverty everywhere in the world, but we have never employed a rational procedure to achieve it. The festering sores of unemployment resulting from increased use of technology, the acceptance of have-not nations in a day when science makes such a condition obsolete, the evil of ignorance when the opportunity for education can be made available to every person on earth—these are not the consequences of the failure of liberalism. The present plight of the world does not testify to the failure of the scientific method. It does speak loudly to the fact that it was never really tried. The problems facing modern man appear to be impossible of resolution, and the appeal to apocalyptic nostrums is not surprising. The revival of faith in moral absolutes and a refurbishing of the doctrine of original sin are psychologically understandable. They are not answers to the problem. The issues before us are not resolved by discrediting reason or promoting spiritual transfiguration. It seems to be more satisfying to utter Jeremiads and prophesy doom than to get at the business of finding answers to vexing problems. Creative despair, it is said, induces faith. It is questionable that it even does that, and if it does, how does it help modern man overcome the threat of an exterminating war!

The times call for a new liberalism, one informed by the new scientific revolution and alive to the fantastic growth of knowledge. What man knows today about the physical universe and himself is extraordinary. The accumulation of information in art, language, anthropology, religion, and philosophy is very impressive. The tragedy of modern man is that he does not use what he knows to help resolve his seemingly unresolvable problems and to enhance the joy and fruitfulness of his life. Liberals themselves are encapsulated today in the shell of nineteenth-century liberalism. They seem to be unaware of new goals undreamed of before and now really possible. For the first time in human history, man is free not only to devise the means to achieve ends set for him by nature or God but he can choose his objectives and direct his course. No human problem may be designated today as inherently ineligible for solution by the scientific method and rational discipline. There is one exception, death.

Let us profile a goal for human existence which will receive general agreement. Better still, let us consider one that has been described for us. "Every individual shall be born a loved and wanted child, in an environment which will, in liberty, allow the full development of all attributes with which he is endowed, physical, mental and spiritual. A continuation of human evolution, both genetic and psychological, such that gradually there may be produced a population in which the many shall possess a stature which is rare indeed today." The criticis of liberalism can add this to their well-stocked collection of testimony convicting it of irrelevance to the condition of modern man. These are pipe dreams, they will charge, that led men astray in the past and brought them to this dreadful hour. Indeed, liberals themselves are unprepared for so radical a proposal. It may be entertained only as a fanciful work of literature. Bellamy's *Looking Backward* was enjoyable reading but not to be taken seriously. The exciting fact of our time is that we can choose this seemingly fantastic goal, knowing that the means of attaining it are at hand. This is what the revolution in human knowledge in our time is all about.

Liberals, historically, make the mistake of setting goals based upon yesterday's knowledge. When, and if, the ideal program is achieved, it is already obsolete since the evolution of the interrelations of man and culture have created a new situation. Liberalism requires a prophetic or poetic imagination to envision the organization of life that is potential in the environment and in human nature. The new genetic studies, for example, break down the last barriers of what man as man can become. Many characteristics of the human organism can be altered. It is realistically possible today, right now, to plan for a future generation which shall be born with the characteristics of wisdom, creativity, stable temperament, and the ability to enjoy life. In 1935 H. J. Muller, Nobel Prize–winning scientist, in projecting this particular goal wrote: "I have carefully considered the problem from the genetic point of view and have come to the reasoned conclusion that all previous serious estimates of the amount of genetic change that could be possible and desirable for man have been too utterly modest." This is no idle dream. The scientist today is not only theorizing, his laboratory reports support his declaration.

Sartre, in a different context, wrote: "Man is condemned at every moment to invent man." Biologically this has become inescapable. Faced with the many staggering problems that arise from a continuous increase in population growth, there are visible first signs of an application of our knowledge toward achieving some control over it. We are moving toward a conscious and planned program of eliminating the element of chance in the size of the world's population by acting on a directive basis. Many social problems which bedevil us today could have been avoided had we not been encapsulated in superstition and ignorance. Birth control is yesterday's goal. The issue now is the nature of human evolution and whether we want to do something about it. Far from having reached the limit of biological evolution, man is at the point where he can give conscious and rational guidance to it. Popular ignorance, social inertia, and fear of reexamining established mores paralyze genuine progress today. Serious proposals of artificial insemination, ectogenesis, rearing the embryo outside the mother's body, are too much even for a liberal mind to entertain.

It is becoming clear that personal love in itself is not a satisfactory vehicle for the needs of reproduction. Thoughts of the future cannot dismiss the possibility of separating them, fettered together though they have been from time immemorial. The knowledge of how to achieve it is at hand. Bold imagination, the hallmark of liberalism, is lacking. A Christian divine, the late Dean Inge, understood it and dared to envision its possibilities for the future. "Eugenics is capable of becoming," he wrote, "the most sacred ideal of the human race; one of the supreme religious duties." The new liberalism can dare to envision planned evolution at the biological and cultural level. It need not wait helplessly for nature to take its slow course, painful and costly as that is.

Freudian analytic psychology is, like Newtonian physics, part of yesterday's noble revolutions. There is increasing evidence that mental illness and irrational behavior are more closely related to organic elements of the human body than to purely psychological experiences. The isolation of particular glandular extractives like insulin, thyroxin, and adrenalin gives us a clue to the possibility of modifying individual constitutions, moods, temperaments, and characters. Dr. Wooley, of the Rockefeller Institute, has experimented with mental defectives and has isolated a basic biochemical deficiency in infancy as its cause. It is now possible to correct this particular abnormality if the treatment is begun at an early stage. What challenges the imagination, however, is Dr. Wooley's speculation that "if a deficiency of serotonin in infancy can have such a deleterious effect on the mind . . . we wonder whether it might be possible to do the reverse and cast some form of super intelligence in this same mold by suitable chemical intervention."

The possibility of improving man's mind permanently is not a wild dream. Responsible scientists soberly project it based on experiments carefully designed and executed. It is now generally accepted that chemical changes alter mental states. It is true, of course, that psychological factors produce mental strain and stress. This, however, means that psychological experiences affect the biomedical composition, which in turn brings on mental disorder. The point is that whether the origin is psychological or not, the cause of mental illness is fundamentally chemical. We are accustomed to "miracle drugs" which cure diseases of the body that only yesterday were seemingly incurable. We are at the threshold of developing "miracle drugs" which promise to cure and prevent mental disabilities and emotional imbalances. It is realistic to project an improvement in the quality of mental power in normal people by an exploration of the chemical nature of the body. Liberalism today may pursue with confidence the goal of the creation of human beings healthier in body and mind.

These are not fantasies. The brooding pessimism which pervades modern culture is powered by yesterday's knowledge. The second law of thermodynamics illustrates the present situation. It projects a future in which all energy will be totally dissipated, and the universe will have reached a dead level of stillness. The prophets of despair point to the steady loss of energy and the ultimate death of the universe as evidence that the earth was never meant to be a place for man to fulfill his hopes. But this is yesterday's physics. Scientists today speak of "Maxwell's demon," a hypothetical entity based on the concept that the energies of the world may gather together at places and occasions. It may be possible to recollect, in usable form, the dissipated entropy of the cosmos. In all probability, this will not affect the plans and programs men devise to improve the conditions of life in the future. It does, however, strike at the mood of despair. "Entropy," wrote J. R. Newman, "is the general trend of the universe toward death and disorder." The new physics says that it is not necessarily so.

The primacy of the historical method in the social and physical sciences has lent credence to the proposition that we know a thing best when we discover its point of origin and trace the story of its development. This often leads to the unwarranted conclusion that the real nature of anything is disclosed in its primitive origin rather than in the form presently achieved. Modern religion is described by some as a means of allaying human fears. Lewis Browne began his volume *This Believing World* with this sentence: "In the beginning was fear." A baby is described by some psychologists as an egocentric creature. The conclusion they draw is that the adult he grows into is self-centered. This naive and false reasoning has crept into much of psychology and philosophy currently taught. It assumes that because man had his origin in the animal kingdom, his real self is essentially animalic, not human.

What is often lost sight of is that man, both as *homo sapiens* and *homo faber*, is a new species, an emergent mutation in the evolution of life. The novelty, which emerged when by chance the new organization of giant molecules created him, is his ability to use symbols and language. This introduced a totally new fact in the evolutionary process—a creature capable of controlling the environment by culture. This is what Dobzhansky calls a "third kind of history," a history of culture superimposed upon cosmic and upon biological evolutionary histories. The ability to use the written and spoken word introduces a critically new form of transmitting the experience of the race from generation to generation. This is man's distinguishing characteristic and the secret of his unique role among the mammals. Insignificant as he appears in size and duration, measured by the vast space-time dimensions of the universe, "he alone," writes Hudson Hoagland, "can experience the thrill of imagination and understanding to a degree not shared by other forms of life. Man's creative imagination is a magnificent emergent of his nervous system.''

Indeed, even as man, he experiences new elements he has never known before. Discoveries in chemistry have revealed new experiences in color; new musical instruments have sensitized the ear to tones unknown in the past; new food, drink, and drugs form part of totally new experiences. The human creature today is different in structure and quality not only from his animal ancestors but even from his early human ancestors. The importance of the story of the evolution of human life lies not in our knowledge of its prehuman origins but in its continuous becoming. New experiences and new discoveries become transformed in man, ever changing him into a new human being. We are not at the end of new discoveries and not, therefore, at the finish line of human development. Those who decry the reality of progress make the mistake of viewing the history of man from the wrong end of the telescope. They set up an ideal goal and measure how far man is from reaching it. They do not measure the distance the race has traveled from the starting point. The distance *from* tells us more about man than the distance *to*.

The new liberalism can start with man as he is known today and begin to throw light upon the potential for growth in his future. The possibilities for dramatic changes and improvements are not limited to his increasing control and exploitation of the physical world. Man has at hand the knowledge and the tools to alter and improve the quality of his own being as a thinking and feeling creature. The new scientific revolution has unencapsulated him. He may, within limits, set any goal and fabricate the means of attaining it. There are limitations—he cannot reverse time. But he can go far indeed. Let those who deny it bring proof.

The cry of despair which dominates the present cultural expression reflects a loss of faith in human destiny. The cataclysmic events of the last half-century have induced in the present generation a failure of nerve. Global wars, persistent revolutions, critical changes in science and society have given rise to philosophies of doom and programs of escape. Serious men pronounce life to be absurd, vain, and senseless. They point an accusing finger, cynically or pitifully, at the illusion of hope which had blinded men of a past generation of enlightenment to the dark reality. The litany is chanted regularly—the earth is not friendly to man's aspirations, men are innately and incorrigibly irrational and wicked, the human creature is by nature an animal who violates the basic principle of his own being when he strives to become human. The prescriptions advanced to relieve such ontological pessimism vary from earthy hedonism to supernatural salvation by grace. Common sense, it seems, has given way to a masochistic reveling in the seamy and absurd elements of human existence.

A major school of modern philosophy turns the searchlight away from the plight and destiny of mankind to the agony and salvation of the individual. Each human life, it is said, is ontologically tragic, doomed existentially to be born alone and to die alone. Truth that matters, meaning that it is real, faith that is relevant begins with the proposition that human existence is by its nature tragic. The individual is counseled to turn his attention from the condition of humankind to the experience of the existential "I". In a day seared by violence, deceit, greed, and brutality, the lure of escapsim and pessimism is almost irresistible. There is just enough truth in the present mood of despair to warrant the attractiveness of a philosophy of pessimism. An individual life, lived for itself alone, measured by the immensity of time and space, may be regarded as insignificant. By himself and for himself, the individual becomes, says H. J. Muller, "a pathetic little journey to death in a universal, vain, struggle."

True enough! One man alone, isolated from the species, will not find significance in his own existence. But man is not alone. It is true that he must die; if he does not die, life on earth will cease. An ancient sage taught that "life is good, death is very good." Without death there can be no life. If all human beings from the beginning of human existence until this hour had not died, life would now be impossible. The given datum of human existence is that man must die, and for whatever it means, he dies alone. This, in itself, is neither tragedy nor a cause for human despair. What is really tragic is that men die who need not and should not. They die in war, from diseases yet unmanageable, from starvation, hatred, and brutality. These deaths need not happen today. The knowledge and the tools are available to eliminate much needless suffering and dying. Pessimistic philosophies which project man's tragic fate do great harm, beside the fact that they are substantially untrue. They entice men to resign themselves to the inevitable tragedy of human existence, permitting, in the meantime, the suffering and agony to continue unrelieved.

There is a fly in the ointment. Is it too late for liberalism? Has the ancient myth been transfigured, compelling Zeus to chain modern Prometheus to the rack? Man has become God. He has the power to create life and to destroy it. He can synthesize macro-molecules in an artificial womb or gather a pool of sperm and mechanically produce a human being. Genetically he knows how to fashion the ideal man, or at least what he considers ideal. Psychologically he knows how to manipulate the mind, to take out of it what he decides should come out and to put in what he determines should be there. He is experimenting with drugs which will ultimately condition man to behave as other men choose for him to behave. He can do better than God—he not only can create life, but he can create a perfect human being as he defines human perfection.

Like the biblical God he can destroy life. He has developed and produced enough destructive weapons to overkill all life on earth many times. Driven by some madness, he is furiously building and storing more and more engines to increase his power to devastate the earth and every living, growing thing in it. Unsatisfied with the thrust of his Tower of Babel into heaven, he has set about to exhaust the resources of the earth while increasing the population that must live on it and off it. The estimates by responsible scholars prophesy that life will not be able to exist on earth if this Malthusian process continues for more than fifty to one hundred years. Changes have been taking place for centuries. Until the present hour they have moved with glacierlike slowness. It has suddenly exploded into the major revolution in human history. It has been said that nature abhors compound interest. The situation of man now is that he can create man, he can destroy man, he can fashion man in his own image, and he can exhaust the nurture of man. Dr. John Von Neumann tells us that "whatever is technologically possible will be done."

The question which takes priority over all others today was asked by the psalmist more than two millennia ago—"What is man?" Endowed with the power to give life and bring death, does he have the wisdom and the benevolence to exercise these in time to avoid the final cataclysm? It appears that man was confronted with this question long ago. Moses before his death said to Israel: "I have set before thee life and death, the blessing and the curse; therefore choose life, that thou mayest live, thou and thy seed." This religious, moral principle, proclaimed as a guide for the conduct of men, has become a terrifying reality demanding an immediate decision. The dominant mood of our culture tends toward despair, the feeling that man cannot mature in sufficient time to choose life. Events in the last several decades give validity to the hopelessness in which modern man agonizes.

Auschwitz and My-Lai give the lie to Shakespeare's benign view of man. "What a piece of work is man! How noble in reason! How infinite in faculty! In form, in moving, how express and admirable! In action how like an angel! In apprehension how like a God! The beauty of the world! The paragon of animals." The present state of human affairs gives support instead to a paraphrase of Shakespeare's encomium of man by J. W. Buckham. "What a piece of work is man! How weak in reason! How powerful in instinct! In form and movement how reflexive and mechanistic! In action how like an ape! In behavior how like an amoeba! The dupe of all the world! The animal of animals!" This is the creature who holds in one hand an ectogenic machine to create life artificially in his own image, and in the other hand the ultimate nuclear weapon to wipe out the last vestige of human existence. What we do not know is the identity of the man. Is he Moses or Pharaoh? Caesar or Jesus? Hitler or Gandhi?

It appears to be too late for a new liberalism. Man not only has the knowledge to eliminate starvation and war but can also biologically and genetically improve his own nature. If there were enough time, he could advance in his own development to the point of maturity to make a decision to sustain life and to enhance it. Two clouds darken the prospect of it happening. Does man possess the moral will and the courage to change his values? Is there sufficient time even if he does? The evidence is rapidly mounting that modern man is living with an apocalyptic expectation. Some unknown event is about to occur which will save him from his doom. A new discovery from the laboratory, a divine miracle in response to faith and prayer, the inventive know-how which brought us the miracles of our magic land, will again dissolve the dark clouds which hang over us. The fallacy of the apocalyptic hope, both divine and natural, is that it rarely arrives in time. The pages of history are bloody with that truth.

While waiting for the miraculous redemption, a strange and paradoxical philosophy of life is being propagated. It represents a mixture of Protestant ethic and high consumption. On the one hand men are urged to work hard, be frugal, practice sobriety, and show sexual restraint. On the other hand man is deluged with propaganda to consume more and more of the earth's resources. The slogan most popular is "You only go around once in this life" so eat more, drink more, and enjoy more. The world is presented as a psychedelic bazaar furnished with three cars, traveled over more and more, and filled with more and more people who buy more, more, and more. The available resources are being exhausted at a rapid pace, the air and the water polluted at an ever higher rate. Confronted with the prophecy that all of this must end in a cataclysm which will make it impossible for life to survive, we echo the king's retort to a similar threat: "Après moi le deluge." We postpone the day and declare: "To hell with our children and grandchildren." This is an apocalyptic time, and the four horsemen are riding fast.

Does the prophetic philosophy of history offer a more believable promise? It proclaims that men, by choosing the right course and committing themselves to just and merciful deeds, can save themselves from destruction. Liberalism, with its reliance upon reason and science, is, in part, an expression of this faith. It has demonstrated during the last two centuries that man can overcome many of the evils which threaten his survival. The new scientific revolution equips him to be master both of nature and human nature. Progress, to paraphrase a commercial on TV, is liberalism's most important achievement. Given enough time we can, in the end of days, beat swords into plowshares and live in prosperity and peace, everyone under his vine and fig tree and none will make them afraid. Unfortunately, there is not enough time. Even the new liberalism, promising as it surely is, cannot turn the present tide against the inevitable catastrophe and avert it.

There are two expressions in the modern world of the prophetic view of history. Both are programmed toward improving the human condition. The oldest, and still vital, may be described as the capitalist, free enterprise, competitive organization in which individualism and personal reward are the dominant characteristics. Its most notable example is the United States, whose dynamic technological development and high standard of living are testimony to the merit of competitive individualism. The natural corollary to this economic arrangement is the belief that every individual is endowed with a natural right to freedom from authority and the right to pursue happiness as he chooses. Other nations in the Western world have prospered under this program, and now Japan has been successful under a similar political-economic system.

The younger, equally vital, modern expression of the prophetic view is Marxism, a society in which the collective needs dominate, and the individual finds his reward in his contribution toward the common good. It is socialistic and at present authoritarian. Individual freedom is subservient to the State, which represents the best interests of all its citizens. The Soviet Union is presently the prominent example of Marxism. It is not now as successful in technological achievement or standard of living as is the United States. But it has, within only a half-century, moved from feudalism to a society which has the scientific knowledge to create nuclear power and industrial technology to satisfy the needs of more people than did the Czarist regime of yesterday. There are other nations who are succeeding under the Marxist program, China especially.

Different from each other as these two programs for the resolution of the problems that trouble men are, they are both derived from the prophetic philosophy of history, not from the apocalyptic. Both have a record of progress which is impressive. Yet both are inadequate as they function today to meet the new phenomena of history—man with more power than God. Capitalism has created great wealth in the hands of very few and varying degrees of poverty for one-third of the nation. It has learned admirably the art of production. It fails miserably with the problem of distribution. The communist society is rapidly growing in its capacity to produce the goods men desire. It does a better job at distribution than capitalism. Capitalism and communism share, however, a critical fallacy which renders both of them helpless in the present situation. Both are committed totally to the greater production and consumption of goods. The aim of Soviet Russia is to catch up with and pass the technological achievement of the United States. Both are on a course of disaster as they furiously exhaust natural resources and pollute the environment. Both neglect the nature of the central figure in this Greek tragedy—man.

Alexander Solzhenitsyn, in one of the most important documents of our time, "Letter to the Soviet Leaders," published in March 1974, has confronted both capitalism and communism with the prophetic dimension which is missing from their economic-political philosophies. Capitalism and communism share with the Hebrew prophets the view that man has the ability to better his lot and move toward utopia. They digress from the prophetic faith on the nature of the utopia. Adam Smith and Karl Marx envisioned the end of days in terms of the consumption of goods. Both understood the ideal human being as the great consumer. They differed on how to achieve this goal, though at one about its nature. Solzhenitsyn tells the

Soviet leaders that Marxism went wrong when it adopted the capitalist definition of human existence. The animosities, wars, hunger, and disaffections which characterize life in both of these societies are atttributable to their materialistic and amoral or immoral character. He calls for confession, repentance, and the doing of good deeds. This is the essence of the prophetic faith, which believes that it takes men regenerated morally and spiritually to save them from destruction.

The now famous Russian author wrote to the leaders of his own country, not to the peoples of the world. The prophets preached to their people Israel, not to all the nations. Solzhenitsyn calls upon his leaders to reverse the direction in which Russia is moving, a highly technical industrial society which searches for world power and colonial satellites. The Russian people do not need two cars in every garage and a television set for every member of the family. They are natural not in huge cities and busy thoroughfares. The beauty of their lives is found in the inward parts, not in the noisy pursuit of more and more things. He is counseling his people to get out of the rat race and live a simple life with nature and themselves. He is asking for a moral and spiritual revolution.

That he did not persuade the Russian leaders comes as no surprise. They did not even respond to his letter. The Russian press denounced him as an enemy of the people, a man who is against the fulfillment of the Communist dream. In the United States he is treated gently and praised warmly for his defense of individual liberty and for the moral and spiritual tone of his life and message. Nobody entertains seriously that it is anything more than what Rousseau and Thoreau have advocated. In fact, there is little or no possibility that man will return to a pre-industrial civilization. Nor is that what Solzhenitsyn is proposing. He is a prophet asking for a radical change in human values. In the face of man's power to create life in his own image and to destroy it all with one blast, the answer may be found in a moral and spiritual regeneration.

The pursuit of the New liberalism cannot and should not be halted. The possibility of devising goals for human existence, and the means to realize them has been opened wide. It is not Ludittism which is needed. Technology in itself is a blessing, not a curse. Man, as a rational creature, will still have to use reason and science to resolve many of his problems. The new issue is the fact that man has vast power and almost no control. The immediate challenge calls for a reexamination of the nature of man. Can he change his goals, his values, his ethics in time to avoid the collapse which seems inevitable? H. G. Wells wrote a story almost a half-century ago about a man who built a perfect stratospheric airplane only to find that sitting behind its wheel was an ape. Is there time now for man to grow in wisdom, grace, justice, and love, to control the unbelievably powerful machine he has constructed?

Consider the life story of one modern man who represents the ideal. It is not fiction. His approach to the goods of the world is to use no more than is barely necessary for existence. In the winter he sets his thermostat at 68, and in the summer at 78. To use more energy is to deny it to those who have little or none. He eats modestly, he dresses neatly, he lives simply. His aim is to do without as much as possible. He is not an ascetic. He is a sensitive human being who is very conscious of so many people on earth who possess nothing and use almost nothing. It will take a world population endowed with those qualities to reverse the human rush toward self-destruction. The possibility of so radical a regeneration of the human creature is very dim. It is more comfortable to escape from the reality of so lowering a prospect into an apocalyptic hope that either God or a superman will save the situation. In conditions not unlike our own, the Hebrew prophets offered one hope—if men do justly, love mercy, and walk humbly they may overcome. Is it too late? This is what Hillel meant when he asked: "If not now, when?"

ABOUT THE CONTRIBUTORS

SAMUEL ATLAS was Professor of Philosophy and Talmud at Hebrew Union College-Jewish Institute of Religion. His field of scientific interest was philosophy and Hebrew law. Among his publications are: *From Critical to Speculative Idealism, The Philosophy of Soloman Maimon 1965; The Contemporary Relevance of Maimonides*. Dr. Atlas has lectured at Cambridge and Oxford.

BERNARD J. BAMBERGER is Rabbi Emeritus of Temple Shaaray Tefila, New York City, and a former president of the Central Conference of American Rabbis. Among his books are *Fallen Angels* and *The Story of Judaism*.

JACK BEMPORAD is Rabbi of Temple Emanu-El, Dallas, Texas and adjunct Professor of Philosophy at Southern Methodist University.

WILLIAM G. BRAUDE, Rabbi emeritus of Temple Beth-El, Providence, Rhode Island, taught at Brown, Providence College, Yale, Hebrew University, Leo Baeck College (London), and University of Connecticut. Among his books are *Midrash on Psalms* (1959), *Pesikta Rabbati* (1968) and *Pesikta dĕ-Raḇ Kahana*.

CARLETON B. CHAPMAN is President of The Commonwealth Fund, a private foundation. He is a physician and was formerly Professor of Medicine at University of Texas Southwestern Medical School (1953-66) and Dean of Dartmouth Medical School (1966-73).

LEON I. FEUER is Rabbi Emeritus of Congregation Shomer Emunim, Sylvania, Ohio of which he was Senior Rabbi for forty years. He has served as President of the Central Conference of American Rabbis; Vice-President of the Zionist Organization of America; and representative of Reform Judaism on the Jewish Agency for Israel. He has been a Visiting Professor at Emory University and the University of Toledo, and is the author of a number of books and essays on Jewish themes.

NORMAN HACKERMAN is an academic administrator and an internationally known chemist in the field of electrochemistry and metal corrosion. He has served as president of Rice University for the past seven years, after 25 years at the University of Texas in Austin in positions from Assistant Professor of Chemistry through the presidency. He is an elected member of the American Philosophical Society, the National Academy of Sciences, and other learned societies, and is presently serving his second term as chairman of the National Science Board.

CHARLES HARTSHORNE is Ashbel Smith Professor Emeritus of Philosophy at The University of Texas at Austin. He has taught at various other universities, including those of Chicago, Melbourne, Emory, and Kyoto. His books include *The Divine Relativity* (1948), *Philosophers Speak of God* (with W. L. Reese, 1953), *Creative Synthesis and Philosophic Method* (1970), *Born to Sing: an Interpretation and World Survey of Birdsong* (1973), *Aquinas to Whitehead: Seven Centuries of Metaphysics of Religion* (1976). He edited (with Paul Weiss, 1931-35) *The Collected Papers of Charles Sanders Peirce.*

GERALD J. KLEIN's association with Temple Emanu-El of Dallas and Levi Olan began in 1952. He was ordained in 1948 and, after serving Temple Gates of Heaven in Schenectady, New York, came to Dallas where he is currently Rabbi of Temple Emanu-El. He is Jewish Chautauqua Society Adjunct Professor at Southern Methodist University.

SCHUBERT M. OGDEN is Professor of Theology in Perkins School of Theology and Director of the Graduate Program in Religion at Southern Methodist University. His best-known writings are *Christ Without Myth: A Study Based on the Theology of Rudolf Bultmann* (1961) and *The Reality of God and Other Essays* (1966; paperback edition, 1977).

SAMUEL SANDMEL is Distinguished Professor at the Hebrew Union College, where he has taught Bible and Hellenistic Jewish Literature. His published Books have been in these areas. He is preparing a new introduction to Philo Judaeus to be published by Oxford University Press.

DAVID SHAKOW is Senior Research Psychologist (1966-   ) at the National Institute of Mental Health and NIH Scientist Emeritus. He was chief Psychologist at the Worcester State Hospital (1928-1946), Professor of Psychology at the University of Illinois and Chicago (1946-1954) and Chief Psychologist at NIH from 1954-1966.

DECHERD TURNER is Professor of Bibliography and Director of Bridwell Library, Southern Methodist University.